Rick Steves®

SNA
P9-ELP-067

Berlin

CONTENTS

INTRODUCTION

This Snapshot guide, excerpted from my guidebook *Rick Steves Germany,* introduces you to the resurgent German capital. Once divided, now reunited, vibrant Berlin is racing into the future as one of Europe's leading cities. Walk under the Brandenburg Gate and stroll up the boulevard called Unter den Linden, pondering the layers of history beneath your feet. Relive the Cold War as you follow the course of the long-gone Berlin Wall, while towering cranes above you erect glittering new skyscrapers. Dip into art museums for a look at classical antiquities and the famous bust of Queen Nefertiti. Then take a day-trip to Frederick the Great's palaces and gardens in Potsdam or the sobering concentration camp memorial at Sachsenhausen.

To help you have the best trip possible, I've included the following topics in this book:

• **Planning Your Time,** with advice on how to make the most of your limited time

• **Orientation,** including tourist information (abbreviated as TI), tips on public transportation, local tour options, and helpful hints

• **Sights** with ratings:

▲▲▲—Don't miss

▲▲—Try hard to see

▲—Worthwhile if you can make it

No rating—Worth knowing about

• **Sleeping** and **Eating,** with good-value recommendations in every price range

• **Connections,** with tips on trains, buses, and driving

Practicalities, near the end of this book, has information on money, staying connected, hotel reservations, transportation, and more, plus German survival phrases.

To travel smartly, read this little book in its entirety before you go. It's my hope that this guide will make your trip more meaningful and rewarding. Traveling like a temporary local, you'll get the absolute most out of every mile, minute, and dollar.

Gute Reise!

Rick Steves

BERLIN

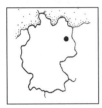

No tour of Germany is complete without a look at its historic and reunited capital. Over the last two decades, Berlin has been a construction zone. Standing on ripped-up tracks and under a canopy of cranes, visitors have witnessed the rebirth of a great European capital. Although construction continues, today the once-divided city is thoroughly woven back together. Berlin has emerged as one of Europe's top destinations: captivating, lively, fun-loving, all-around enjoyable—and easy on the budget.

Of course, Berlin is still largely defined by its tumultuous 20th century. The city was Hitler's capital during World War II, and in the postwar years, it became the front line of a new global war—one between Soviet-style communism and American-style capitalism. The East-West division was set in stone in 1961, when the East German government boxed in West Berlin with the Berlin Wall. The Wall stood for 28 years. In 1990, less than a year after the Wall fell, the two Germanys—and the two Berlins—officially became one. When the dust settled, Berliners from both sides of the once-divided city faced the monumental challenge of reunification.

Throughout the Cold War, Western travelers—and most West Berliners—got used to thinking of western Berlin and its Kurfürstendamm boulevard as the heart of the city. With the huge changes the city has undergone since 1989, the real "city center" is now, once again, Berlin's historic center (the Mitte district, around Unter den Linden and Friedrichstrasse).

When the Wall came down, the East was a decrepit wasteland and the West was a paragon of commerce and materialism. Urban planners seized on the city's reunification and the return of the national government to make Berlin a great capital once again. Now,

BERLIN

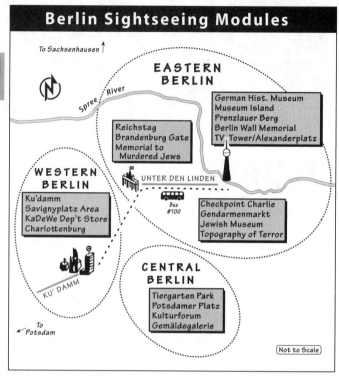

Berlin Sightseeing Modules

To Sachsenhausen ↑

EASTERN BERLIN

Spree River

German Hist. Museum
Museum Island
Prenzlauer Berg
Berlin Wall Memorial
TV Tower/Alexanderplatz

Reichstag
Brandenburg Gate
Memorial to
Murdered Jews

WESTERN BERLIN

UNTER DEN LINDEN

Ku'damm
Savignyplatz Area
KaDeWe Dep't Store
Charlottenburg

Bus #100

Checkpoint Charlie
Gendarmenmarkt
Jewish Museum
Topography of Terror

KU' DAMM

CENTRAL BERLIN

Tiergarten Park
Potsdamer Platz
Kulturforum
Gemäldegalerie

To Potsdam

Not to Scale

a quarter-century later, the old "East Berlin" is where you feel the vibrant pulse of the city, while the old "West Berlin" has the feel of a chic, classy suburb. Berliners joke that they don't need to travel anywhere because their city's always changing. Spin a postcard rack to see what's new. A 10-year-old guidebook on Berlin covers a different city.

But even as the city busily builds itself into the 21st century, Berlin has made a point of acknowledging and remembering its past. A series of thought-provoking memorials installed throughout the city center—chief among them the Memorial to the Murdered Jews of Europe—directly confront some of Germany's most difficult history of the last century. Lacing these sights into your Berlin sightseeing intensifies your understanding of the city and its past.

As you walk over what was the Wall and through the well-patched Brandenburg Gate, it's clear that history is not contained in some book; it's an evolving story in which we play a part. In Berlin, the fine line between history and current events is excitingly blurry.

But even for non-historians, Berlin is a city of fine experiences. Explore the fun and funky neighborhoods in the former East, packed with creative hipster eateries and boutiques trying to one-up each other. Go for a pedal or a cruise along the delightful Spree riverfront. In the city's world-class museums, walk through an enormous Babylonian gate amid rough-and-tumble ancient statuary, and peruse canvases by Dürer, Rembrandt, and Vermeer. Nurse a stein of brew in a rollicking beer hall, or dive into a cheap *Currywurst*.

Berlin today is the nuclear fuel rod of a great nation. It's vibrant with youth, energy, and an anything-goes-and-anything's-possible buzz (Munich feels spent in comparison). And it's a magnet for a young international crowd—who have overtaken some neighborhoods in such huge numbers that many expats get by just fine without knowing much German. Berlin is both extremely popular and surprisingly affordable. As a booming tourist draw, Berlin now welcomes more visitors annually than Rome.

PLANNING YOUR TIME

On all but the shortest trips through Germany, I'd give Berlin three nights and at least two full days, and spend them this way:

Day 1: Begin your day getting oriented to this huge city. For a quick and relaxing once-over-lightly tour, jump on one of the many hop-on, hop-off buses that make two-hour narrated orientation loops through the city. Use the bus to get off and on at places of interest (such as Potsdamer Platz). Then walk from the Reichstag (reservations required to climb its dome), under the Brandenburg Gate, and down Unter den Linden following my "Best of Berlin" self-guided walk. Tour the German History Museum, and cap your sightseeing day by catching a one-hour boat tour (or pedaling a rented bike) along the park-like banks of the Spree River from Museum Island to the Chancellery.

Day 2: Spend your morning touring the great museums on Museum Island (note that the Pergamon Museum's famous altar is out of view until 2019). Dedicate your afternoon to sights of the Third Reich and Cold War: After lunch, hike to the Topography of Terror exhibit and along the surviving Niederkirchnerstrasse stretch of the Wall to Checkpoint Charlie. Head to the Berlin Wall Memorial for a more in-depth survey of that infamous barrier, or swing by the Jewish Museum. Finish your day in the lively Prenzlauer Berg district.

Berlin merits additional time if you have it. There's much more in the city (such as the wonderful Gemäldegalerie art museum). And nearby are some very worthwhile day trips: At Potsdam, glide like a swan through the opulent halls of an imperial palace or, at Oranienburg, ponder the darkest chapter of this nation's past at the Sachsenhausen Concentration Camp Memorial. The historic town

The History of Berlin

Berlin was a humble, marshy burg—its name perhaps derived from an old Slavic word for "swamp"—until prince electors from the Hohenzollern dynasty made it their capital in the mid-15th century. Gradually their territory spread and strengthened, becoming the powerful Kingdom of Prussia in 1701. As the leading city of Prussia, Berlin dominated the northern Germanic world—both militarily and culturally—long before there was a united "Germany."

The only Hohenzollern ruler worth remembering was Frederick the Great (1712-1786). The ultimate enlightened despot, he was both a ruthless military tactician (he consolidated his kingdom's holdings, successfully invading Silesia and biting off a chunk of Poland) and a cultured lover of the arts (he actively invited artists, architects, and other thinkers to his lands). "Old Fritz," as he was called, played the flute, spoke six languages, and counted Voltaire among his friends. Practical and cosmopolitan, Frederick cleverly invited to Prussia Protestants who were being persecuted elsewhere in Europe—including the French Huguenots and Dutch traders. Prussia became the beneficiary of these groups' substantial wealth and know-how. Frederick the Great left Berlin—and Prussia—a far more modern and enlightened place than he found it. Thanks largely to him, Prussia was well-positioned to become a magnet of sorts for the German unification movement in the 19th century.

When Germany first unified, in 1871, Berlin (as the main city of its most powerful constituent state, Prussia) was its natural capital. Even in the disarray of post-WWI Germany, Berlin thrived as an anything-goes, cabaret-crazy cultural capital of the Roaring

of Wittenberg—less than an hour away by train—is gearing up for the 500th birthday of the Reformation in 2017.

Orientation to Berlin

Berlin is huge, with 3.4 million people. The city is spread out and its sights numerous, so you'll need to be well-organized to experience it all smartly. The tourist's Berlin can be broken into three main digestible chunks:

Eastern Berlin has the highest concentration of notable sights and colorful neighborhoods. Near the landmark Brandenburg Gate, you'll find the Reichstag building, Pariser Platz, and

'20s. During World War II, the city was Hitler's headquarters—and the place where the Führer drew his final breath. When the Soviet Army reached Berlin in 1945, the protracted fighting left the city in ruins.

After World War II, Berlin was divided by the victorious Allied powers. The American, British, and French sectors became West Berlin, and the Soviet sector, East Berlin. In 1948 and 1949, the Soviets tried to starve the 2.2 million residents of the Western half in an almost medieval-style siege, blockading all roads in and out. But they were foiled by the Berlin Airlift, with the Western Allies flying in supplies from Frankfurt 24 hours a day for 10 months.

Years later, with the overnight construction of the Berlin Wall in 1961, an Iron (or, at least, concrete) Curtain literally cut through the middle of the city, completely encircling West Berlin—for details, see "The Berlin Wall (and Its Fall)" on page 66.

While the wild night when the Wall came down (November 9, 1989) was inspiring, Berlin still faced a fitful transition to reunification. Two cities—and countries—became one at a staggering pace. Reunification had its downside, and the Wall survives in the minds of some people. Some "Ossies" (impolite slang for Easterners) missed their security. Some "Wessies" missed their easy ride (military deferrals, subsidized rent, and tax breaks for living in an isolated city surrounded by the communist world). For free spirits, walled-in West Berlin was a citadel of freedom within the East.

More than 25 years later, the old East-West division has faded. The city government has been eager to charge forward, with little nostalgia for anything associated with the East. Big corporations and the national government have moved in, and the dreary swath of land that was the Wall and its notorious "death strip" has been transformed (as the cash-starved city has been selling off lots of land to anyone determined to develop it). Berlin is a whole new city—ready to welcome visitors.

poignant memorials to Hitler's victims. From the Brandenburg Gate, the famous Unter den Linden boulevard runs eastward, passing the German History Museum and Museum Island (Pergamon Museum, Neues Museum, and Berlin Cathedral) on the way to Alexanderplatz (TV Tower). South of Unter den Linden are the delightful Gendarmenmarkt square, noteworthy Nazi sites (including the Topography of Terror), good Wall-related sights (Museum of the Wall at Checkpoint Charlie), and the Jewish Museum. Farther south is the colorful Kreuzberg neighborhood. Across the Spree River are the worth-a-wander neighborhoods of Hackescher Markt, Oranienburger Strasse, and Prenzlauer Berg (recommended hotels and a very lively restaurant/nightlife zone).

The Berlin Wall Memorial is at the west edge of Prenzlauer Berg. The stretch of the Wall known as the East Side Gallery is to the east, beyond Alexanderplatz in the burgeoning district of Friedrichshain.

Central Berlin is dominated by the giant Tiergarten park, with its angel-topped Victory Column. South of the park are the German Resistance Memorial, Potsdamer Platz, and the Kulturforum museum complex, which includes the Gemäldegalerie, New National Gallery (closed until at least 2017), Musical Instruments Museum, and Philharmonic Concert Hall. To the north is the huge Hauptbahnhof (the city's main train station), with the Natural History Museum nearby.

Western Berlin focuses on the Bahnhof Zoo train station (often marked "Zoologischer Garten" on transit maps) and the grand Kurfürstendamm boulevard, nicknamed "Ku'damm" (transportation hub, shopping, and recommended hotels). Even though the east side of the city is all the rage, big-name stores and destination restaurants keep the west side buzzing. During the Cold War, capitalists visited this "Western Sector," possibly with a nervous side-trip beyond the Wall into the grim and foreboding East. (Cubans, Russians, Poles, and Angolans stayed behind the Wall and did their sightseeing in the East.)

TOURIST INFORMATION

With any luck, you won't have to use Berlin's TIs—they're for-profit agencies working for the city's big hotels, which colors the information they provide. TI branches, appropriately called "info-stores," are unlikely to have the information you need (tel. 030/250-025, www.visitberlin.de). You'll find them at the **Hauptbahnhof** train station (daily 8:00-22:00, by main entrance on Europaplatz), at **Europa Center** (Mon-Sat 10:00-20:00, closed Sun, hidden inside shopping mall ground floor at Tauentzienstrasse 9; nearby "info box" kiosk on Rankestrasse across from **Kaiser Wilhelm Memorial Church** open daily 10:00-18:00, until 16:00 Nov-March), at the **Brandenburg Gate** (daily 9:30-19:00, until 18:00 Nov-March), and at the **TV Tower** (daily 10:00-18:00, until 16:00 Nov-March, Panoramastrasse 1a).

Skip the TI's €1 map, and instead browse the walking tour company brochures—many include nearly-as-good maps for free. Most hotels also provide free city maps. While the TI does sell the three-day Museum Pass Berlin (described next), it's also available at major museums. If you take a walking tour, your guide is likely a better source of nightlife or shopping tips than the TI.

Museum Passes: The three-day, €24 **Museum Pass Berlin** is a great value and pays for itself in a hurry. It gets you into more than 50 museums, including the national museums and most of the recommended biggies (though not the German History Museum), on three consecutive days. Sights covered by the pass include the five Museum Island museums (Old National Gallery, Neues, Altes, Bode, and Pergamon), Gemäldegalerie, and the Jewish Museum Berlin, along with other more minor sights. Buy it at the TI or any participating museum. The pass generally lets you skip the line and go directly into the museum.

The €18 **Museum Island Pass** (Bereichskarte Museumsinsel; does not include special exhibits) covers all the venues on Museum Island and is a fine value—but for just €6 more, the three-day Museum Pass Berlin gives you triple the days and many more entries. TIs also sell the **WelcomeCard,** a transportation pass that includes discounts for the following recommended sights (and more): Berlin Cathedral, DDR Museum, German History Museum, Museum of the Wall at Checkpoint Charlie, Jewish Museum Berlin, and The Kennedys Museum (pass described later, under "Getting Around Berlin").

ARRIVAL IN BERLIN
By Train at Berlin Hauptbahnhof

Berlin's grandest train station is Berlin Hauptbahnhof (a.k.a. "der Bahnhof", abbreviated Hbf). All long-distance trains arrive here,

at Europe's biggest, mostly underground train station. This is a "transfer station"—unique for its major lines coming in at right angles—where the national train system meets the city's S-Bahn trains.

The gigantic station can be intimidating, but it's laid out logically on five floors (which, confusingly, can be marked in different ways). Escalators and elevators connect the **main floor** (*Erdgeschoss,* EG, a.k.a level 0); the two **lower levels** (*Untergeschoss,* UG1 and UG2, a.k.a. levels -1 and -2); and the two **upper levels** (*Obersgeschoss,* OG1 and OG2, a.k.a. levels +1 and +2). Tracks 1-8 are in the lowest underground level (UG2), while tracks 11-16 (along with the S-Bahn) are on the top floor (OG2). Shops and services are concentrated on the three middle levels (EG, OG1, and UG1). The south entrance (toward the Reichstag and downtown, with a taxi stand) is marked *Washingtonplatz,* while the north entrance is marked *Europaplatz.*

Services: On the main floor (EG), you'll find the **TI** (facing the north/*Europaplatz* entrance, look left) and the **"Rail & Fresh WC"** facility (public pay toilets, near the Burger King and food court). Up one level (OG1) are a 24-hour **pharmacy** and **lockers** (directly under track 14).

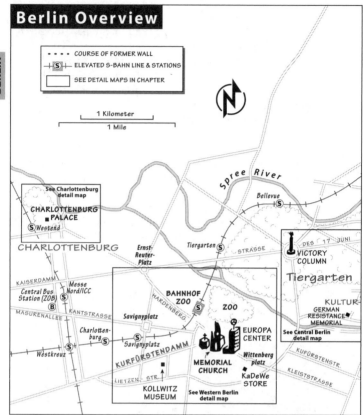

Train Information and Tickets: The station has a Deutsche Bahn *Reisezentrum* information center on the first upper level (OG1/+1, open long hours daily). If you're staying in western Berlin, keep in mind that the info center at the Bahnhof Zoo station is just as good and much less crowded.

EurAide is an English-speaking information desk with answers to your questions about train travel around Europe. It's located at counter 12 inside the *Reisezentrum* on the first upper level (OG1/+1). It's American-run, so communication is simple. This is an especially good place to make fast-train and *couchette* reservations (generally open Mon-Fri 10:30-19:00, until 20:00 May-July and Sept, check website for specific hours, closed Jan-Feb and Sat-Sun year-round; www.euraide.com).

Shopping: In addition to all those trains, the Hauptbahnhof is home to 80 shops with long hours—some locals call the station a "shopping mall with trains" (only stores selling travel provisions are open Sun). The Kaisers supermarket (UG1, follow signs for tracks 1-2) is handy for assembling a picnic for your train ride.

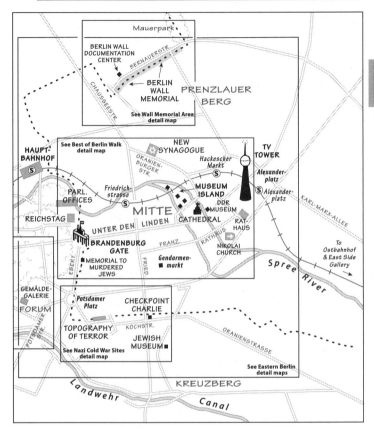

Getting into Town: Taxis and buses wait outside the station, but the S-Bahn is probably the best means of connecting to your destination within Berlin. It's simple: All S-Bahn trains are on tracks 15 and 16 at the top of the station (level OG2/+2). All trains on track 15 go east, stopping at Friedrichstrasse, Hackescher Markt (with connections to Prenzlauer Berg), Alexanderplatz, and Ostbahnhof; trains on track 16 go west, toward Bahnhof Zoo and Savignyplatz. (Your train ticket or rail pass into the station covers your connecting S-Bahn ride into town; your outbound ticket includes the transfer via S-Bahn to the Hauptbahnhof.)

To reach most recommended hotels in eastern Berlin's Prenzlauer Berg neighborhood, it's fastest to take any train on track 15 two stops to Hackescher Markt, exit to Spandauer Strasse, go left, and cross the tracks to the tram stop. Here you'll catch tram #M1 north (direction: Schillerstrasse).

To reach western Berlin, catch any train on track 16 to Savignyplatz, where you're a five-minute walk to most recommended hotels. Savignyplatz is one stop after **Bahnhof Zoo** (rhymes with "toe"; a.k.a. Bahnhof Zoologischer Garten), the once-grand train hub now eclipsed by the Hauptbahnhof. Nowadays Bahnhof Zoo is an unusually sketchy S-Bahn stop; expect it to be a massive construction zone.

The Berlin Hauptbahnhof is not well-connected to the city's U-Bahn (subway) system—yet. The station's sole U-Bahn line—U55—goes only two stops, to the Brandenburger Tor station, and doesn't really connect to the rest of the system. It's part of a planned extension of the U5 line to Alexanderplatz that's far from completion. But for transit junkies, it is an interesting ride on Europe's shortest subway line.

By Plane

For information on reaching the city center from Berlin's airports, see "Berlin Connections" at the end of this chapter.

HELPFUL HINTS

Medical Help: "**Call a doc**" is a nonprofit referral service designed for tourists (tel. 01805-321-303, phone answered 24 hours a day, www.call-a-doc.com). The US Embassy also has a list of local English-speaking doctors (tel. 030/83050, http://germany.usembassy.gov).

Museum Tips: Some major Berlin museums are closed on Monday. If you plan to see several museums, you'll save money with the Museum Pass Berlin, which covers nearly all the city sights for three days—including everything covered by the one-day Museum Island Pass (see "Tourist Information—Museum Passes," earlier).

Addresses: Many Berlin streets are numbered with odd and even numbers on the same side of the street, often with no connection to the other side (for example, Ku'damm #212 can be across the street from #14). To save steps, check the white street signs on curb corners; many list the street numbers covered on that side of the block.

Festivals: Berlin hosts a near-constant string of events, including the **Berlinale** international film festival (11 days in February, www.berlinale.de), **Carnival of Cultures** (four-day street festival of international music and dance culminating in a parade through Kreuzberg's Blücherplatz on Pentecost Sunday, www.karneval-berlin.de), **Classic Open Air Festival** (six days of music on Gendarmenmarkt, early July, www.classicopenair.de), **International Literature Festival** (everything presented in its original language, 10 days in September, www.literaturfestival.com), big celebrations around the Brandenburg Gate for **Unity Day** (October 3), **Festival of Lights** (landmark buildings artistically lit for a week in mid-October, www.festival-of-lights.de), and **Jazzfest Berlin** (four days in early November, www.berlinerfestspiele.de).

Cold War Terminology: What Americans called "East Germany" was technically the German Democratic Republic—the Deutsche Demokratische Republik, or DDR (pronounced day-day-AIR). You'll still see those initials around what was once East Germany. The name for what was "West Germany"—the Federal Republic of Germany (Bundesrepublik Deutschland, or BRD)—is now the name shared by all of Germany.

Laundry: Berlin has several self-service launderettes with long hours (wash and dry-€4-9/load). Near my recommended hotels in Prenzlauer Berg, try **Waschsalon 115** (daily 6:00-22:00, Wi-Fi, Torstrasse 115, around corner from recommended Circus hostel) or **Eco-Express Waschsalon** (daily 6:00-22:00, handy pizzeria next door, Danziger Strasse 7). The **Schnell & Sauber Waschcenter** chain has a location in Prenzlauer Berg (daily 6:00-23:00, Oderberger Strasse 1).

Local Publications: *Berlin Programm* is a comprehensive German-language monthly, especially strong in high culture, that lists upcoming events and museum hours (€2.20, www.berlin-programm.de). *Exberliner Magazine,* an English monthly (published mostly by expat Brits who love to poke fun at expat Americans), gives a fascinating insider's look at this fast-changing city (€3 but often given away at theaters or on the street, www.exberliner.com).

Shell Games: Believe it or not, there are still enough idiots on the street to keep the con men with their shell games in business. Don't be foolish enough to engage with any gambling on the street.

Updates to This Book: For the latest, check www.ricksteves.com/update.

GETTING AROUND BERLIN

The city is vast. Berlin's sights spread far and wide. Right from the start, commit yourself to the city's fine public-transit system.

By Public Transit: Subway, Train, Tram, and Bus

Berlin's consolidated transit system uses the same ticket for its many modes of transportation: U-Bahn (*Untergrund-Bahn,* Berlin's subway), S-Bahn (*Stadtschnellbahn,* or "fast urban train," mostly

BERLIN

aboveground), *Strassenbahn* (tram), and bus. For all types of transit, there are three lettered zones (A, B, and C). Most of your sightseeing will be in zones A and B (the city proper)—but you'll need to buy a ticket that also covers zone C if you're going to Potsdam, Sachsenhausen, Schönefeld airport, or other outlying areas.

Berlin's public transit is operated by BVG (except the S-Bahn, which is run by the Deutsche Bahn). Timetables and the latest prices are available on the helpful BVG website (www.bvg.de). Get and use the excellent *Discover Berlin by Train and Bus* map-guide published by BVG (at subway ticket windows).

Ticket Options

- The €2.70 **basic single** ticket *(Einzelfahrschein)* covers two hours of travel in one direction. It's easy to make this ticket stretch to cover several rides...as long as they're in the same direction.

- The €1.60 **short-ride** ticket *(Kurzstrecke Fahrschein)* covers a single ride of up to six bus/tram stops or three subway stations (one transfer allowed on subway). You can save a little bit on short-ride tickets by buying them in groups of four (€5.60).

- The €9 **four-trip** ticket *(4-Fahrten-Karte)* is the same as four basic single tickets at a small discount.

- The **day pass** *(Tageskarte)* is good until 3:00 the morning after you buy it (€6.90 for zones AB, €7.40 for zones ABC). For longer stays, consider a seven-day pass *(Sieben-Tage-Karte;* €29.50 for zones AB, €36.50 for zones ABC), or the WelcomeCard (options from 2 to 6 days; described below). The *Kleingruppen-karte* lets groups of up to five travel all day (€16.90 for zones AB, €17.40 for zones ABC).

- If you've already bought a ticket for zones A and B, and later decide that you want to go to zone C (such as to Potsdam), you can buy an **"extension ticket"** *(Anschlussfahrschein)* for €1.60 per ride in that zone.

- If you plan to cover a lot of ground using public transportation during a two- or three-day visit, the **WelcomeCard** is usually the best deal (available at TIs; www.visitberlin.de/welcomecard). It covers all public transportation and gives you up to 50 percent discounts on lots of minor and a few major museums (including Checkpoint Charlie), sightseeing tours (including 25 percent off the recommended Original Berlin Walks), and music and theater events. It's especially smart for families, as each adult card also covers up to three kids under age 15. The Berlin-only card covers transit zones AB (€19.50/48 hours, €27.50/72 hours, also 4-, 5-, and 6-day options). For multiple trips beyond the city center, there's a Berlin-with-Potsdam card (zones ABC, €21.50/48 hours, €29.50/72 hours, also 4-, 5-, and 6-day options). If you're a museum junkie, consider the **WelcomeCard+Museumsinsel** (€42/72 hours), which combines travel in zones A and B with unlimited access to the five museums on Museum Island (€44/72 hours for the ABC version).

Buying Tickets: You can buy U-Bahn/S-Bahn tickets from machines at stations. (They are also sold at BVG pavilions at train stations and at the TI, from machines on board trams, and on buses from drivers, who'll give change.) *Erwachsener* means "adult"—anyone age 14 or older. Don't be afraid of the automated machines: First select the type of ticket you want, then load the coins or paper bills. (Coins work better, so keep some handy.)

Boarding Transit: As you board the bus or tram, or enter the subway, punch your ticket in a clock machine to validate it (or risk a €60 fine; for passes, stamp it only the first time you ride). Be sure to travel with a valid ticket. Tickets are checked frequently, often by plainclothes inspectors. You may be asked to show your ticket when boarding the bus (technically that's required), though most drivers skip this.

Transit Tips: The S-Bahn crosstown express is a river of public transit through the heart of the city, in which many lines converge on one basic highway. Get used to this, and you'll leap within a few minutes between key locations: Savignyplatz (hotels in western Berlin), Bahnhof Zoo (Ku'damm, bus #100), Hauptbahnhof (all major trains in and out of Berlin), Friedrichstrasse (a short walk north of the heart of Unter den Linden; this station has the interesting Palace of Tears exhibit), Hackescher Markt (Museum Island, restaurants, nightlife, connection to Prenzlauer Berg hotels and eateries), and Alexanderplatz (eastern end of Unter den Linden).

Sections of the U-Bahn or S-Bahn sometimes close temporarily for repairs. In this situation, a bus route often replaces the train (*Ersatzverkehr*, or "replacement transportation"; *zwischen* means "between").

Within Berlin, Eurail passes are good only on S-Bahn connections from the train station when you arrive and to the station when you depart.

By Taxi

Cabs are easy to flag down, and taxi stands are common. A typical ride within town costs €8-10, and a crosstown trip (for example, Savignyplatz to Alexanderplatz) will run about €15. Tariff 1 is for a *Kurzstrecke* ticket (see below). All other rides are tariff 2 (€3.40 drop plus €1.80/km for the first 7 kilometers, then €1.28/km after that). If possible, use cash—paying with a credit card comes with a hefty surcharge (about €4, regardless of the fare).

Money-Saving Taxi Tip: For any ride of less than two ki-

lometers (about a mile), you can save several euros if you take advantage of the *Kurzstrecke* (short-stretch) rate. To get this rate, it's
important that you flag the cab down on the street—not at or even
near a taxi stand. You must ask for the *Kurzstrecke* rate as soon as
you hop in: Confidently say *"Kurzstrecke, bitte"* (KOORTS-shtreh-
keh, BIT-teh), and your driver will grumble and flip the meter to a
fixed €4 rate (for a ride that would otherwise cost €7).

By Bike

Flat Berlin is a very bike-friendly city, but be careful—Berlin's
motorists don't brake for bicyclists (and bicyclists don't brake for
pedestrians). Fortunately, some roads
and sidewalks have special red-paint-
ed bike lanes. Don't ride on the regular sidewalk—it's *verboten* (though
locals do it all the time). Better yet, to
get out of the city on two wheels, rent
a bike, take it on the subway (requires
extra €1.80 ticket) to the pleasant
Potsdam/Wannsee parkland area
west of town, then ride through forests and along skinny lakes to
the vast Grünewald park, then back into the city. (During the Cold
War, Grünewald was the Wessies' playground, while Ossies com-
muned with nature at the Müggelsee, east of town.) Bike shops can
suggest a specific route.

Fat Tire Bikes rents good bikes at two handy locations—East
(at the base of the TV Tower near Alexanderplatz) and West (at
Bahnhof Zoo—leaving the station onto Hardenbergplatz, turn left
and walk 100 yards to the big bike sign). Both locations have the
same hours and rates (€14/day, cheaper rate for two or more days,
trekking and e-bikes available, free luggage storage, daily May-
Aug 9:30-20:00, March-April and Sept-Oct 9:30-18:00, shorter
hours or by appointment only Nov-Feb, leave ID, tel. 030/2404-
7991, www.berlinbikerental.com).

In eastern Berlin, **Take a Bike**—near the Friedrichstrasse S-
Bahn station—is owned by a lovely Dutch-German couple who
know a lot about bikes and have a huge inventory (3-gear bikes:
€8/4 hours, €12.50/day, €19/2 days, slightly cheaper for longer
rentals, more for better bikes, includes helmets, daily 9:30-19:00,
Neustädtische Kirchstrasse 8, tel. 030/2065-4730, www.takeabike.
de). To find it, leave the S-Bahn station via the Friedrichstrasse
exit, turn right, go through a triangle-shaped square, and hang a
left on Neustädtische Kirchstrasse.

All around town, simple **Rent a Bike** stands are outside count-
less shops, restaurants, and hotels. Most charge €10 to €12 a day,
and are super-convenient, given their ubiquitous availability—but

these bikes don't come with the reliable quality, advice, helmets, or maps commonly offered by full-service rental shops.

Tours in Berlin

BUS TOURS

▲▲▲Hop-On, Hop-Off Buses

Several companies offer the same routine: a circuit of the city with unlimited hop-on, hop-off privileges all day for about €20 (about 15 stops at the city's major tourist spots—Potsdamer Platz, Museum Island, Brandenburg Gate, the Kaiser Wilhelm Memorial Church, and so on). For specifics, look for brochures in your hotel lobby or at the TI. Buses come with cursory narration in English and German by a live, sometimes tired guide or a boring recorded commentary. In season, buses run at least four times per hour. They are great for photography—and Berlin really lends itself to this kind of bus-tour orientation.

Before handing over the money, consider following my self-guided "City Bus #100 tour" instead (below), which costs only the price of a transit ticket. If you do opt for the commercial route, go with a live guide rather than the recorded spiel (buses generally run April-Oct daily 10:00-18:00, departures every 10 minutes, last bus leaves all stops at around 16:00, 2-hour loop; Nov-March 2/hour and last departure at 15:00).

BEX Sightseeing Berlin

This company offers a long list of bus tours (including hop-on, hop-off) in and around Berlin; their 2.5-hour "City Circle Yellow" tour is a good introduction. You can hop on and off at any of 18 stops, or simply stay on for the full tour (1 day-€20, 2 days-€24, 6/hour April-Oct daily 10:00-18:00, Fri-Sat until 19:00; Nov-March daily until 17:00; recorded English commentary, departs from Ku'damm 216, buy ticket on bus or from S-Bahn machines and ticket windows, tel. 030/880-4190, www.berlinerstadtrundfahrten.de).

City Bus #100

For do-it-yourselfers, Berlin's city bus #100 is a cheap, quick, workable alternative to the commercial hop-on, hop-off bus tours—and you can follow along with my self-guided bus tour.

▲▲▲WALKING TOURS

Berlin's fascinating and complex history can be challenging to appreciate on your own, making the city an ideal place to explore with a walking tour. Equal parts historian and entertainer, a good Berlin tour guide makes the city's dynamic story come to life.

Unlike many other European countries, Germany has no regulations controlling who can give city tours. This can make

Berlin at a Glance

▲▲▲**German History Museum** The ultimate swing through Germany's tumultuous story. **Hours:** Daily 10:00-18:00. See page 54.

▲▲▲**Pergamon Museum** World-class museum of classical antiquities on Museum Island, partially closed through 2019 (including its famous Pergamon Altar). **Hours:** Daily 10:00-18:00, Thu until 20:00. See page 49.

▲▲▲**Reichstag** Germany's historic parliament building, topped with a striking modern dome you can climb (reservations required). **Hours:** Daily 8:00-24:00, last entry at 22:00. See page 23.

▲▲▲**Brandenburg Gate** One of Berlin's most famous landmarks, a massive columned gateway, at the former border of East and West. **Hours:** Always open. See page 27.

▲▲▲**Berlin Wall Memorial** A "docu-center" with videos and displays, several outdoor exhibits, and lone surviving stretch of an intact Wall section. **Hours:** Visitor Center Tue-Sun 10:00-18:00, closed Mon; outdoor areas accessible 24 hours daily. See page 75.

▲▲**Memorial to the Murdered Jews of Europe** Holocaust memorial with almost 3,000 symbolic pillars, plus an exhibition about Hitler's Jewish victims. **Hours:** Memorial always open; information center open Tue-Sun 10:00-20:00, Oct-March until 19:00, closed Mon. See page 30.

▲▲**Unter den Linden** Leafy boulevard through the heart of former East Berlin, lined with some of the city's top sights. **Hours:** Always open. See page 33.

▲▲**Neues Museum** Egyptian antiquities collection (on Museum Island) and proud home of the exquisite 3,000-year-old bust of Queen Nefertiti. **Hours:** Daily 10:00-18:00, Thu until 20:00. See page 50.

▲▲**Gendarmenmarkt** Inviting square bounded by twin churches (one with a fine German history exhibit), a chocolate shop, and a concert hall. **Hours:** Always open. See page 57.

▲▲**Topography of Terror** Chilling exhibit documenting the Nazi perpetrators, built on the site of the former Gestapo/SS headquarters. **Hours:** Daily 10:00-20:00. See page 60.

▲▲**Museum of the Wall at Checkpoint Charlie** Kitschy but moving museum with stories of brave Cold War escapes, near the former site of the famous East-West border checkpoint; the surrounding street scene is almost as interesting. **Hours:** Daily 9:00-22:00. See page 64.

▲▲**Jewish Museum Berlin** Engaging, accessible museum celebrating Jewish culture, in a highly conceptual building. **Hours:** Daily 10:00-20:00, Mon until 22:00. See page 65.

▲▲**DDR Museum** Quirky collection of communist-era artifacts. **Hours:** Daily 10:00-20:00, Sat until 22:00. See page 56.

▲▲**Gemäldegalerie** Germany's top collection of 13th- through 18th-century European paintings, featuring Holbein, Dürer, Cranach, Van der Weyden, Rubens, Hals, Rembrandt, Vermeer, Velázquez, Raphael, and more. **Hours:** Tue-Fri 10:00-18:00, Thu until 20:00, Sat-Sun 11:00-18:00, closed Mon. See page 85.

▲▲**Prenzlauer Berg** Lively, colorful neighborhood with hip cafés, restaurants, boutiques, and street life. **Hours:** Always open. See page 73.

▲**Old National Gallery** German paintings, mostly from the Romantic Age. **Hours:** Tue-Sun 10:00-18:00, Thu until 20:00, closed Mon. See page 52.

▲**New Synagogue** Largest prewar synagogue in Berlin, damaged in World War II, with a rebuilt facade and modest museum. **Hours:** April-Oct Mon-Fri 10:00-18:00, Sun until 19:00; Oct-March exhibit only Sun-Thu 10:00-18:00, Fri until 15:00; closed Sat year-round. See page 72.

▲**Potsdamer Platz** The "Times Square" of old Berlin, long a postwar wasteland, now rebuilt with huge glass skyscrapers, an underground train station, and—covered with a huge canopy—the Sony Center mall. **Hours:** Always open. See page 82.

▲**Deutsche Kinemathek Film and TV Museum** An entertaining look at German film and TV, from *Metropolis* to Dietrich to Nazi propaganda to the present day. **Hours:** Tue-Sun 10:00-18:00, Thu until 20:00, closed Mon. See page 83.

▲**Kaiser Wilhelm Memorial Church** Evocative destroyed church in heart of the former West Berlin, with modern annex. **Hours:** Church—daily 9:00-19:00; Memorial Hall in bombed tower—Mon-Fri 10:00-18:00, Sat 10:00-17:30, shorter hours Sun. See page 91.

▲**Käthe Kollwitz Museum** The black-and-white art of the Berlin artist who conveyed the suffering of her city's stormiest century. **Hours:** Daily 11:00-18:00. See page 93.

guide quality hit-or-miss, ranging from brilliant history buffs who've lived in Berlin for years while pursuing their PhDs, to new arrivals who memorize a script and start leading tours after being in town for just a couple of weeks. To improve your odds of landing a great guide, use one of the companies I recommend in this section.

Most outfits offer walks that are variations on the same themes: general **introductory** walk, **Third Reich** walk (Hitler and Nazi sites), and day trips to **Potsdam** and the **Sachsenhausen Concentration Camp Memorial**. Most tours cost about €12-15 and last about three to four hours (longer for the side-trips to Potsdam and Sachsenhausen); public-transit tickets and entrances to sights are extra. For details—including prices and specific schedules—see each company's website or look for brochures in town (widely available at TIs, hotel reception desks, and many cafés and shops).

Brewer's Berlin Tours

Specializing in longer, more in-depth walks that touch on the entire span of Berlin's past, this company was started by the late, great Terry Brewer, who once worked for the British diplomatic service in East Berlin. Terry left the company to his guides, a group of historians who get very excited about Berlin. Their city tours are intimate, relaxed, and can flex with your interests. Their Best of Berlin introductory tour, billed at six hours, can last for eight (daily at 10:30). They also do a shorter 3.5-hour tour (free, tip expected, daily at 13:00) and an all-day Potsdam tour (Wed and Sat, May-Oct). All tours depart from Bandy Brooks ice cream shop at the Friedrichstrasse S-Bahn station (mobile 0177-388-1537, www.brewersberlintours.com).

Insider Tour

This well-regarded company runs the full gamut of itineraries: introductory walk (daily), Third Reich, Cold War, Jewish Berlin, alternative culture, Sachsenhausen, and Potsdam, as well as pub crawls and a day trip to Dresden. Their tours have two meeting points: in the West at the McDonald's across from Bahnhof Zoo, and in the East at AM to PM Bar at the Hackescher Markt S-Bahn station (tel. 030/692-3149, www.insidertour.com).

Original Berlin Walks

Their flagship introductory walk, Discover Berlin, offers a good overview in four hours (daily year-round, meet at 10:00 at Bahnhof Zoo, April-Oct also daily at 13:30). They also offer a Third Reich walking tour; themed walks on topics such as Jewish Life in Berlin, Cold War Berlin, and Queer Berlin; and tours to Potsdam, Sachsenhausen, and Wittenberg. Readers of this book get a €1 discount per tour in 2016. Tours depart from the taxi stand in front of the Bahnhof Zoo train station or opposite the Hackescher Markt S-Bahn station, outside the Weihenstephaner restaurant (tour info: tel. 030/301-9194, www.berlinwalks.de).

BERLIN

Berlin Underground Association (Berliner Unterwelten Verein)

Much of Berlin's history lies beneath the surface, and this group has an exclusive agreement with the city to explore and research what is hidden underground. Their one-of-a-kind Dark Worlds tour takes you into a WWII air-raid bunker (Thu-Sun at 11:00 and Mon at 11:00 and 13:00). The "From Flak Towers to Mountains of Debris" tour enters the Humboldthain air defense tower (April-Oct Thu-Tue at 11:00). The "Subways and Bunkers in the Cold War" tour visits a fully functional nuclear emergency bunker in former West Berlin (Thu-Sun at 13:00). Additional tour times and days are added in summer; check online (most tours cost €11 and last about 1.5 hours). Meet in the hall of the Gesundbrunnen U-Bahn/S-Bahn station—follow signs to the *Humboldthain/Brunnenstrasse* exit, and walk up the stairs to their office (tel. 030/4991-0517, www.berliner-unterwelten.de).

Alternative Berlin Tours

Specializing in cutting-edge street culture and art, this company emphasizes the bohemian chic that flavors the city's ever-changing urban scene. Their basic three-hour tour (daily at 11:00, 13:00, and 15:00) is tip-based; other tours cost €12-20 (all tours meet at Starbucks on Alexanderplatz under the TV Tower, mobile 0162-819-8264, www.alternativeberlin.com).

"Free" Tours

You'll see companies advertising supposedly "free" introductory tours all over town. Designed for and popular with students (free is good), it's a business model that has spread across Europe: English-speaking students (often Aussies and Americans) deliver a memorized script before a huge crowd lured in by the promise of a free tour. Tour leaders expect to be "tipped in paper" (€5 minimum per person is encouraged). While the guides can be highly entertaining, the better ones typically move on to more serious tour companies before long. These tours are fine for poor students with little interest in real history. But as with many things, when it comes to walking tours, you get what you pay for.

The "free" tour companies also offer **pub crawls** that are wildly popular with visiting college students.

Local Guides

Berlin guides are generally independent contractors who work with the various tour companies (such as those listed here). Many guides are Americans who came to town as students and history buffs, fell in love with Berlin, and now earn their living sharing their city. Some lead private tours on their own (generally charging around €50-60/hour or €200-300/day, confirm when booking). The following guides are all good: **Nick Jackson** (an archaeologist and historian who makes museums come to life, mobile 0171-537-8768, www.jacksonsberlintours.com, info@jacksonsberlintours.com, nick.jackson@berlin.de); **Lee Evans** (makes 20th-century Germany a thriller, mobile 0177-423-5307, lee.evans@berlin.de); **Bernhard Schlegelmilch** (an enthusiastic historian who grew up behind the Wall, mobile 0176-6422-9119, www.steubentoursberlin.com, info@steubentoursberlin.com), and **Holger Zimmer** (a journalist and cultural connoisseur who also guides my groups, mobile 0163-345-4427, explore@berlin.de).

BIKE TOURS
Fat Tire Bike Tours
Choose among five different tours, which run (except where noted) from April through October (most €28, 4-6 hours, 6-10 miles): **City Tour** (April-Sept daily at 10:00, 11:00, and 16:00; Oct daily at 10:00 and 11:00; March and Nov daily at 11:00; Dec-Feb Wed and Sat at 11:00), **Berlin Wall Tour** (Mon and Thu-Sun at 10:30), **Third Reich Tour** (Wed and Fri-Sun at 10:30), **"Raw" Tour** (countercultural, creative aspects of contemporary Berlin, Tue, Fri, and Sun at 10:30), and **Gardens and Palaces of Potsdam Tour** (€46, Wed and Fri-Sun at 9:45). For any tour, meet at the TV Tower at Alexanderplatz (reserve ahead except for City Tour, tel. 030/2404-7991, www.fattirebiketours.com).

BOAT TOURS
Spree River Cruises
Several boat companies offer one-hour, €13 trips up and down the river. In one relaxing hour, you'll listen to excellent English audioguides, see lots of wonderful new government-commissioned architecture, and enjoy the lively park action fronting the river. Boats leave from various docks that cluster near the bridge at the Berlin Cathedral (just off Unter den Linden). For better  views, I'd go for a two-story boat with open-deck seating. I enjoyed the Historical Sightseeing Cruise from **Stern und Kreisschiffahrt** (mid-March-Nov daily 10:00-19:00, leaves from Nikolaiviertel Dock—cross bridge from Berlin Cathedral toward Alexanderplatz

City Bus #100 Tour

Running from Bahnhof Zoo to Alexanderplatz, Berlin's city bus #100 laces together the major sights in a kind of poor man's self-guided bus tour. As a basic, single bus ticket is good for two hours of travel in one direction and buses leave every few minutes, hopping on and off works great. Bus #100 stops at Bahnhof Zoo train station, the Berlin Zoo, the Victory Column, the Reichstag, Unter den Linden, the Brandenburg Gate, the Pergamon Museum, and Alexanderplatz.

Here's a quick review of what you'll see: Leaving from the Bahnhof Zoo train station, you'll spot the bombed-out hulk of the **Kaiser Wilhelm Memorial Church,** with its jagged spire and postwar sister church. Then, on the left, the elephant gates mark the entrance to the venerable and much-loved **Berlin Zoo** and its aquarium. After a left turn, you cross the canal and pass Berlin's **embassy row.**

The bus then enters the vast 400-acre **Tiergarten** city park, once a royal hunting ground and now packed with cycling paths, joggers, and—on hot days—nude sunbathers. Straight ahead, the **Victory Column** (Siegessäule; with the gilded angel) towers above. A block beyond the Victory Column (on the left) is the 18th-century late-Rococo **Bellevue Palace,** the residence of the federal president (if the flag's out, he's in).

Driving along the Spree River (on the left), you'll see several striking **national government** buildings. A metal Henry Moore sculpture entitled *Butterfly* (a.k.a. "The Drinker's Liver") floats in front of the slope-roofed House of World Cultures. Through the trees on the left is the **Chancellery**—Germany's "White House." The big open space is the **Platz der Republik,** where the Victory Column (which you passed earlier) stood until Hitler moved it. The Hauptbahnhof (Berlin's vast main train station, marked by its tall tower with the *DB* sign) is across the field between the Chancellery and the **Reichstag** (Germany's parliament—the old building with the new dome).

Hop off at the next stop (Reichstag/Bundestag) if you'd like to follow my "Best of Berlin Walk." But if you stay on the bus, you'll zip by the next string of sights, in this order:

Unter den Linden, the main east-west thoroughfare, stretches from the **Brandenburg Gate** through Berlin's historic core to the TV Tower in the distance. You'll pass the **Russian Embassy** and the Aeroflot airline office (right). Crossing **Friedrichstrasse,** look right for a Fifth Avenue-style conga line of big, glitzy department stores. Later, on the left, are the **German History Museum, Museum Island**, and the **Berlin Cathedral;** across from these (on the right) is the construction site of the **Humboldt-Forum Berliner Schloss** (with the Humboldt-Box visitors center). You'll rumble to a final stop at the transit hub of **Alexanderplatz.**

and look right, tel. 030/536-3600, www.sternundkreis.de). Confirm that the boat you choose comes with English commentary.

TOUR PACKAGES FOR STUDENTS

Andy Steves (my son) runs **Weekend Student Adventures** (WSA
Europe), offering three-day and longer guided and unguided pack-
ages—including accommodations, sightseeing, and unique local
experiences—for student travelers in 12 top European cities, including Berlin (guided trips from €199, see www.wsaeurope.com).

Best of Berlin Walk

This two-mile self-guided walk, worth ▲▲▲, starts in front of the
Reichstag, takes you under the Brandenburg Gate and down Unter
den Linden, and finishes on Alexanderplatz, near the TV Tower. I
describe minor sights along the way, and also point out major ones
that you'll want to visit later or by taking a break from the walk
(find their details later in this chapter, under "Sights in Eastern
Berlin"). If you have just one day in Berlin, or want a good orientation to the city, simply follow this walk (two-three hours at a brisk
pace, not counting museum visits). By the end, you'll have seen the
core of Berlin and its most important sights.

If you have more time and want to use this walk as a spine for
your sightseeing, entering sights and museums as you go, consider
doing Part 1 and Part 2 on different days. Part 1 goes from the
Reichstag and takes you partway down Unter den Linden, with
stops at the Brandenburg Gate, Memorial to the Murdered Jews
of Europe, and Friedrichstrasse, the glitzy shopping street. Part 2
continues down Unter den Linden, from Bebelplatz to Alexanderplatz, and features Museum Island and the Spree River, the Berlin
Cathedral, and the iconic TV Tower.

∩ Download my free Berlin Walk audio tour, which narrates
the route and sights described next.

PART 1: THE REICHSTAG TO UNTER DEN LINDEN

During the Cold War, the Reichstag stood just inside the West
Berlin side of the Wall. Even though it's been more than 25 years
since the Wall came down, you may still feel a slight tingle down
your spine as you walk across the former death strip, through the
once *verboten* Brandenburg Gate, and into the former communist
east.

• *Start your walk directly in front of the Reichstag building, at the big,
grassy park called...*

❶ Platz der Republik

Stand about 100 yards in front of the grand Reichstag building and spin left to survey your surroundings. At the **Reichstag U-Bahn stop** is a big federal building overlooking the Spree River. The huge **main train station** *(Hauptbahnhof)* is in the distance (see the tower marked *DB,* for Deutsche Bahn—the German rail company). Farther left is the mammoth white concrete-and-glass **Chancellery,** nicknamed the "washing machine" by Berliners for its hygienic, spin-cycle appearance. It's the office of Germany's most powerful person, the chancellor (currently Angela Merkel). To remind the chancellor whom he or she works for, Germany's Reichstag (housing the parliament) is about six feet taller than the Chancellery.

Beyond the Chancellery is the Spree River. When kings ruled Prussia, government buildings crowded right up to its banks. But today, the riverscape is a people-friendly zone (we'll see it later on this walk).

• *Dominating the Platz der Republik is a giant domed building, the...*

❷ Reichstag

The parliament building—the heart of German democracy and worth ▲▲▲—has a short but complicated and emotional his-

tory. When it was inaugurated in the 1890s, the last emperor, Kaiser Wilhelm II, disdainfully called it the "chatting home for monkeys" *(Reichsaffenhaus).* It was placed outside the city's old walls—far from the center of real power, the imperial palace. But it was from the Reichstag that the German Republic was proclaimed in 1918. Look above the door, surrounded by stone patches from WWII bomb damage, to see the motto and promise: *Dem Deutschen Volke* ("To the German People").

In 1933, this symbol of democracy nearly burned down. The Nazis—whose influence on the German political scene was on the rise—blamed a communist plot. A Dutch communist, Marinus van der Lubbe, was eventually convicted and guillotined for the crime. Others believed that Hitler himself planned the fire, using it as a handy excuse to frame the communists and grab power. Even though Van der Lubbe was posthumously pardoned by the German government in 2008, most modern historians concede that he most likely was guilty, and had acted alone—the timing was just incredibly fortuitous for the Nazis, who shrewdly used his deed to advance their cause.

The Reichstag was hardly used from 1933 to 1999. Despite the fact that the building had lost its symbolic value, Stalin ordered his troops to take the Reichstag from the Nazis no later than May 1,

BERLIN

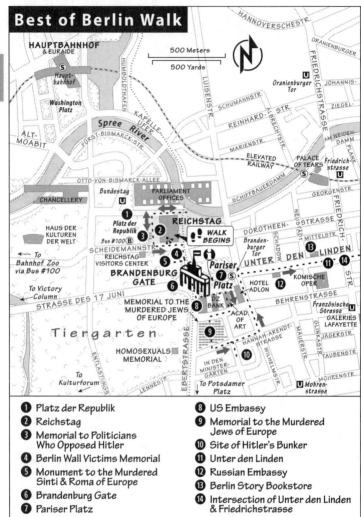

Best of Berlin Walk

1. Platz der Republik
2. Reichstag
3. Memorial to Politicians Who Opposed Hitler
4. Berlin Wall Victims Memorial
5. Monument to the Murdered Sinti & Roma of Europe
6. Brandenburg Gate
7. Pariser Platz
8. US Embassy
9. Memorial to the Murdered Jews of Europe
10. Site of Hitler's Bunker
11. Unter den Linden
12. Russian Embassy
13. Berlin Story Bookstore
14. Intersection of Unter den Linden & Friedrichstrasse

1945 (the date of the workers' May Day parade in Moscow). More than 1,500 Nazi soldiers made their last stand here—extending World War II by two days. On April 30, after fierce fighting on its rooftop, the Reichstag fell to the Red Army.

For the building's 101st birthday in 1995, the artist-partners Christo and Jeanne-Claude wrapped the entire thing in silvery gold cloth. It was then wrapped again—in scaffolding—and rebuilt by British architect Lord Norman Foster into the new parliamentary home of the Bundestag (Germany's lower house, similar to the US House of Representatives). In 1999, the German parliament convened here for the first time in 66 years. To many Germans, the

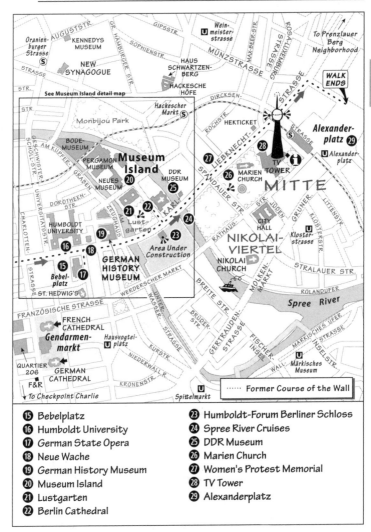

15 Bebelplatz	**23** Humboldt-Forum Berliner Schloss
16 Humboldt University	**24** Spree River Cruises
17 German State Opera	**25** DDR Museum
18 Neue Wache	**26** Marien Church
19 German History Museum	**27** Women's Protest Memorial
20 Museum Island	**28** TV Tower
21 Lustgarten	**29** Alexanderplatz
22 Berlin Cathedral	

proud resurrection of the Reichstag symbolizes the end of a terrible chapter in their country's history.

The **glass cupola** rises 155 feet above the ground. Its two sloped ramps spiral 755 feet to the top for a grand view. Inside the dome, a cone of 360 mirrors reflects natural light into the legislative chamber below. Illuminated from inside after dark, this gives Berlin a memorable nightlight. The environmentally friendly cone—with an opening at the top—also helps with air circulation, expelling stale air from the legislative chamber (no joke) and pulling in fresh, cool air.

Visitors with advance reservations can climb the spiral ramp

BERLIN

up into the cupola. If you haven't booked a slot, you can cross the street to the white booth to check available entry times.

• *Face the Reichstag and walk to the right. Near the road in front of the building, enmeshed in all the security apparatus and crowds, is a memorial of slate stones embedded in the ground.*

❸ Memorial to Politicians Who Opposed Hitler

This row of slabs, which looks like a fancy slate bicycle rack, is a memorial to the 96 members of the Reichstag who were persecuted and murdered because their politics didn't agree with Chancellor Hitler's. They were part of the Wei-

mar Republic, the weak and ill-fated attempt at post-WWI democracy in Germany. These were the people who could have stopped Hitler...so they became his first victims. Each slate slab memorializes one man—his name, party (mostly KPD—Communists, and SPD—Social Democrats), and the date and location of his death—generally in a concentra-

tion camp (indicated by *"KZ"* on the slabs). They are honored here, in front of the building in which they worked.

• *Walk along the side of the Reichstag, on busy Scheidemannstrasse, toward the rear of the building. At the intersection with Ebertstrasse, cross to the right (toward the park). Along a railing is a small memorial of white crosses. This is the...*

❹ Berlin Wall Victims Memorial

This monument commemorates some of the East Berliners who died trying to cross the Wall. Many of them perished within months of the Wall's construction on August 13, 1961. Most died trying to swim the Spree River to freedom. This monument used to

stand right on the Berlin Wall behind the Reichstag. The last person killed while trying to escape was 20-year-old Chris Gueffroy, who was shot through the heart in no-man's land nine months before the Wall fell in 1989.

• *Continue along Ebertstrasse for*

BERLIN

a few more steps and turn into the peaceful lane on the right (into leafy Tiergarten park). Within a short distance, on your right, is the...

❺ Monument to the Murdered Sinti and Roma (Gypsies) of Europe

Unveiled in 2012, this memorial remembers the roughly 500,000 Sinti and Roma victims of the Holocaust. "Sinti" and "Roma" (the main tribes and politically correct terms for the group more commonly called "Gypsies") were as persecuted by the Nazis as were the Jews. And they lost the same percentage of their population to Hitler. The opaque glass wall, with a timeline in English and German, traces the Nazi abuse and atrocities.

Enter through the rusty steel portal. On the other side is a circular reflecting pool surrounded by stone slabs, some containing the names of the death camps where hundreds of thousands of Sinti and Roma perished. In the water along the rim of the pool is the heart-wrenching poem "Auschwitz," by composer and writer Santino Spinelli, an Italian Roma. Dissonant music evoking the tragedy of the Sinti and Roma genocide adds to the atmosphere.

• *Retrace your steps to Ebertstrasse and turn right, toward the busy intersection dominated by the imposing Brandenburg Gate. Take this chance to get oriented. Behind you, as you face the Brandenburg Gate, is* **Tiergarten park**, *its center marked by the landmark Victory Column.*

Now face the Brandenburg Gate. It stands at one end of Unter den Linden, the Champs-Elysées of Berlin. In the distance, the red-and-white spire of the TV Tower marks the end of this walk.

Cross the street toward the gate, and notice the double row of cobblestones beneath your feet—it goes about 25 miles around the city, marking where the Wall used to stand. Then walk under the gate that, for a sad generation, was part of a wall that divided this city.

❻ Brandenburg Gate (Brandenburger Tor)

The historic ▲▲▲ Brandenburg Gate (1791) was the grandest—and is the last survivor—of 14 gates in Berlin's old city wall (this one led to the neighboring city of Brandenburg). The gate was

the symbol of Prussian Berlin—and later the symbol of a divided Berlin. It's crowned by a majestic four-horse chariot, with the Goddess of Peace at the reins. Napoleon took this statue to the Louvre in Paris in 1806. After the Prussians defeated Napoleon and got it back (1813), she was renamed the Goddess of Victory.

The Brandenburg Gate, Arch of Peace

More than 200 years ago, the Brandenburg Gate was designed as an arch of peace, crowned by the Goddess of Peace and showing Mars sheathing his sword. The Nazis misused it as a gate of triumph and aggression. Today a Room of Silence, built into the gate, is dedicated to the peaceful message of the original Brandenburg Gate. As you consider the history of Berlin in this silent and empty room—which is carefully not dedicated to any particular religion—you may be inspired to read the prayer of the United Nations:

"Oh Lord, our planet Earth is only a small star in space. It is our duty to transform it into a planet whose creatures are no longer tormented by war, hunger, and fear, no longer senselessly divided by race, color, and ideology. Give us courage and strength to begin this task today so that our children and our children's children shall one day carry the name of man with pride."

The gate sat unused, part of a sad circle dance called the Berlin Wall, for more than 25 years. Now postcards all over town show the ecstatic day—November 9, 1989—when the world rejoiced at the sight of happy Berliners jamming the gate like flowers on a parade float. Pause a minute and think about struggles for freedom—past and present. (There's actually a special room built into the gate for this purpose—see the sidebar.) There's also a TI within the gate. Around the gate, information boards show how this area changed throughout the 20th century.

The gate sits on a major boulevard running east to west through Berlin. The western segment, called Strasse des 17 Juni (named for a workers' uprising against the DDR government on June 17, 1953), stretches for four miles from the Brandenburg Gate, through the Tiergarten, past the Victory Column, to the Olympic Stadium. But we'll follow this city axis in the opposite direction—east, along Unter den Linden into the core of old imperial Berlin, and past the site where the palace of the Hohenzollern family, rulers of Prussia and then Germany, once stood. The royal palace is a phantom sight, long gone, but its occupants were responsible for just about all you'll see.

• *Pass all the way through the gate and stand in the middle of...*

❼ Pariser Platz

"Parisian Square," so named after the Prussians defeated Napoleon in 1813, was once filled with important government buildings—all bombed to smithereens in World War II. For decades, it was an unrecognizable, deserted no-man's-land—cut off from both East and West by the Wall. Banks, hotels, and embassies have now reclaimed their original places on the square (worth ▲)—with a few additions, including a palace of coffee, Starbucks. The winners of World War II enjoy this prime real estate: The American, French, British, and Russian embassies are all on or near this square.

As you face the gate, to your right is the French Embassy, and to your left is the ❽ **US Embassy,** which reopened in its historic pre-WWII location in 2008. (While Germany was divided, the embassy relocated to Bonn, with only a "mission" in West Berlin, as the US refused to officially recognize Berlin as the capital of East Germany.) For safety's sake, Uncle Sam wanted more of a security zone around the building, but the Germans wanted to keep Pariser Platz a welcoming people zone. The compromise: Extra security was built into the structure. Easy-on-the-eyes barriers keep potential car bombs at a distance, and the front door is on the side farthest from the Brandenburg Gate.

Turn your back to the gate. On the right, jutting into the square, is the ritzy **Hotel Adlon,** long called home by visiting stars and VIPs. In its heyday, it hosted such notables as Charlie Chaplin, Albert Einstein, and Greta Garbo. It was the setting for Garbo's most famous line, "I vant to be alone," uttered in the film *Grand Hotel.* Damaged by the Russians just after World War II, the original hotel was closed when the Wall went up in 1961 and later demolished. Today's grand Adlon was rebuilt in 1997. It was here that Michael Jackson shocked millions by dangling his infant son over a balcony railing.

• *Between the hotel and the US Embassy are two buildings worth a quick visit: the DZ Bank building and the glassy Academy of Arts. We'll enter both, then leave Pariser Platz through the Academy of Arts.*

DZ Bank Building: This building's architect, Frank Gehry, is famous for Bilbao's Guggenheim Museum, Prague's Dancing House, Seattle's Experience Music Project, Chicago's Pritzker Pavilion, and Los Angeles' Walt Disney Concert Hall. Gehry fans might be surprised at the bank building's low profile. Structures on Pariser Platz are designed so as not to draw attention away from the Brandenburg Gate. But to get your fix of wild and colorful Gehry, step into the lobby. Built in 2001 as an office complex and conference center, its undulating interior is like a big, slithery fish. Gehry explained, "The form of the fish is the best example of movement. I try to capture this movement in my buildings."

• *Leaving the DZ Bank, turn right and head into the next building, the...*

Academy of Arts (Akademie der Künste): The glassy arcade is open daily (WC in basement, café serves light meals). Just past the café is the office where Albert Speer, Hitler's architect, planned the rebuilding of postwar Berlin into "Welthauptstadt Germania"—the grandiose "world capital" of Nazi Europe. Pass through the glass door to see Speer's favorite statue, *Prometheus Bound* (c. 1900). This is the kind of art that turned Hitler on: a strong, soldierly, vital man, enduring hardship for a greater cause. Anticipating the bombing of Berlin, Speer had the statue bricked up in the basement here where it lay, undiscovered, until 1995.

This building provides a handy and interesting passage to the Holocaust memorial on the other side.

• *Exit the building out the back. Across the street, to the right, stretches the vast...*

❾ Memorial to the Murdered Jews of Europe (Denkmal für die Ermordeten Juden Europas)

Completed in 2005, this Holocaust memorial (worth ▲▲) consists of 2,711 gravestone-like pillars called "stelae." Designed by Jewish-American architect Peter Eisenman, it was Germany's first formal, government-sponsored Holocaust memorial. Using the word "murdered" in the title was intentional and a big deal. Germany, as a nation, was officially admitting to a crime.

Cost and Hours: The memorial is free and always open. The information center is open Tue-Sun 10:00-20:00, Oct-March until 19:00, closed Mon year-round; last entry 45 minutes before closing, entry involves brief security screening, S-Bahn: Brandenburger Tor or Potsdamer Platz, tel. 030/2639-4336, www.stiftung-denkmal.de. A €4 audioguide augments the experience.

Visiting the Memorial: The pillars, made of hollow concrete, stand in a gently sunken area, which can be entered from any side. The number of pillars isn't symbolic of anything; it's simply how many fit on the provided land. The pillars are all about the same size, but of differing heights. The memorial's location—where the Wall once stood—is coincidental. Nazi propagandist Joseph Goebbels' bunker was discovered during the work and left buried under the northeast corner of the memorial.

Once you enter the memorial, notice that people seem to appear and disappear between the columns, and that no matter where you are, the exit always seems to be up. The memorial is thoughtfully lit at night and guarded.

The monument was criticized for focusing on just one of the groups targeted by the Nazis, but the German government has now erected memorials to other victims—such as the Roma/Sinti memorial we just visited, and a memorial to the regime's homosexual victims, also nearby. It's also been criticized because there's nothing intrinsically Jewish about it. Some were struck that there's no central gathering point or place for a ceremony. Like death, you enter it alone.

There is no one intended interpretation. Is it a symbolic cemetery, or an intentionally disorienting labyrinth? It's up to the visitor to derive the meaning, while pondering this horrible chapter in human history.

Memorial Information Center: The pondering takes place under the sky. For the learning, go under the field of concrete pil-

lars to the state-of-the-art information center. Inside, an excellent and thought-provoking exhibit (well-explained in English) studies the Nazi system of extermination and personalizes the plight of victims; there's also space for silent reflection. In the first hall, exhibits trace the historical context of the Nazi and WWII era, while six portraits—representing the six million Jewish victims—look out on visitors. The next room has glowing boxes in the floor containing diaries, letters, and final farewells penned by Holocaust victims. A third room presents case studies of 15 Jewish families from around Europe, to more fully convey the European Jewish experience. Behind these 15 stories are millions more tales of despair, tragedy, and survival. In the most somber part of the center, a continually running soundtrack reads the names and brief biographies of Holocaust victims. The final room of the exhibit documents some 220 different places of genocide. You'll also find exhibits about other Holocaust monuments and memorials, a searchable database of victims, and a video archive of interviews with survivors.

• *Wander through the gray pillars, but eventually emerge on the corner with the Information Center. Cross Hannah-Arendt-Strasse and go a half block farther. Walk alongside the rough parking lot (on the left side of street) to the info plaque over the...*

❿ Site of Hitler's Bunker

You're standing atop the buried remains of the *Führerbunker*. In early 1945, as Allied armies advanced on Berlin and Nazi Germany lay in ruins, Hitler and his staff retreated to a bunker complex behind the former Reich Chancellery. He stayed there for two months. It was here, as the Soviet army tightened its noose on the capital, that Hitler and Eva Braun, his wife of less than 48 hours, committed suicide on April 30, 1945. A week later, the war in Eu-

Imagining Hitler in the 21st Century

Now seven decades after the end of World War II, the bunker where Hitler killed himself lies hidden underneath a Berlin parking lot. While the Churchill War Rooms are a major sight in London, no one wants to turn Hitler's final stronghold into a tourist attraction.

Germans tread lightly on their past. It took 65 years for the Germany History Museum to organize its first exhibit on the life of Hitler. Even then, the exhibit was careful not to give neo-Nazis any excuse to celebrate—even the size of the Hitler portraits was kept to a minimum.

The image of Hitler has been changing in Germany. No longer is he exclusively an evil mass murderer; sometimes he is portrayed as a nervous wreck or as an object of derision. He's even a wax figure in the Berlin branch of Madame Tussauds.

But 21st-century Germans still treat the subject with extraordinary sensitivity. The Bavarian state hasn't allowed any version of *Mein Kampf,* Hitler's political manifesto, to be published in German within Germany, even one annotated by historians. Any visit to Hitler's mountain retreat in Berchtesgaden includes a stop at the Nazi Documentation Center, where visitors see Nazi artifacts carefully placed in their historical context.

Many visitors to Berlin are curious about Hitler sites, but not much survives from that dark period. The German Resistance Memorial is worthwhile, but not really geared toward non-German visitors (see page 81). Hitler's bunker is marked only by a small information board. The best way to learn about Hitler sites is to take a Third Reich tour offered by one of the many local walking-tour companies (see "Tours in Berlin," page 15), or to visit the Topography of Terror, a fascinating exhibit located where the SS and Gestapo headquarters once stood (see page 60).

It's a balancing act, and Germans are still in the process of figuring out how to confront their painful past.

rope was over. The info board presents a detailed cutaway illustrating the bunker complex plus a timeline tracing its history and ultimate fate (the roof was removed and the bunker filled with dirt, then covered over).

• *From here, you can visit the important but stark Memorial to the Homosexuals Persecuted Under the National Socialist Regime, or you can continue the walk. To do either, first head back to Hannah-Arendt-Strasse.*

To see the **memorial** *(it's a bit of a detour), go left one block at Hannah-Arendt-Strasse, cross the street, and head down a path into Tiergarten park. There, look for a large, dark gray concrete box. Through a* *small window you can watch a film loop of same-sex couples kissing—a reminder that life and love are precious.*

*To rejoin the **walk**, turn right on Hannah-Arendt-Strasse, go one block, then head left up Wilhelmstrasse. Because Wilhelmstrasse was a main street of the German government during WWII, it was obliterated by bombs, and all its buildings are new today. The pedestrianized part of the street is home to the British Embassy. The fun, purple color of its wall is the colors of the Union Jack mixed together.*

Back on Unter den Linden, head to the median, in front of Hotel Adlon, and take a long look down...

⓫ Unter den Linden

In the good old days, this ▲▲ street was one of Europe's grand boulevards. In the 15th century, it was a carriageway leading from

the palace to the hunting grounds (today's big Tiergarten). In the 17th century, Hohenzollern princes and princesses moved in and built their palaces here so they could be near the Prussian king. It is divided, roughly at Friedrichstrasse, into a business section, which stretches toward the Brandenburg Gate, and a cultural section, which spreads out toward Alexanderplatz. Frederick the Great wanted to have culture, mainly the opera and the university, closer to his palace and to keep business (read: banks) farther away, near the city walls.

Named centuries ago for its thousands of linden trees, this was the most elegant street of Prussian Berlin before Hitler's time, and the main drag of East Berlin after his reign. Hitler replaced the venerable trees—many 250 years old—with Nazi flags. Popular discontent drove him to replant the trees. Later, Unter den Linden deteriorated into a depressing Cold War cul-de-sac, but it has long since regained its strolling café ambience.

• In front of Hotel Adlon is the Brandenburger Tor S-Bahn station. Cover a bit of Unter den Linden underground by climbing down its steps and walking along the platform.

Ghost Subway Station: The Brandenburger Tor S-Bahn station is one of Berlin's former ghost subway stations. During the Cold War, most underground train tunnels were simply sealed at the border. But a few Western lines looped through the East and then back into the West. To make a little hard

Western cash, the Eastern government rented the use of these tracks to the West. For 28 years, as Western trains passed through otherwise blocked-off stations, passengers saw only eerie East German guards and lots of cobwebs. Within days of the fall of the Wall, these stations reopened (one woman who'd left her purse behind in 1961 got a call from the lost-and-found office—it was still there). Today they are a time warp, looking much as they did when built in 1931, with dreary old green tiles and original signage on ticket kiosks.

• *Walk along the track (the walls are lined with historic photos of the Reichstag through the ages) and exit on the other side, to the right. You'll pop out at the Russian Embassy's front yard.*

🔟 **Russian Embassy:** This was the first big postwar building project in East Berlin. It's in the powerful, simplified Neoclassical style that Stalin liked. While not as important now as it was a few years ago, it's as immense as ever. It flies the Russian white, blue, and red. On the median out front, you may well see protesters speaking out against Russia's latest questionable action—or, just as likely, in defense of it. Find the hammer-and-sickle motif decorating the window frames—a reminder of the days when Russia was the USSR.

• *At the next intersection (Glinkastrasse), cross to the other side of Unter den Linden. At #40 is the...*

🔟 **Berlin Story Bookstore:** Berlin Story is two shops side by side (on the left it's mainly Cold War souvenirs; on the right, the bookstore). The bookshop has just about the best range anywhere of English-language titles on Berlin (Mon-Sat 10:00-19:00, Sun until 18:00). They also run a little museum at a separate location.

• *A few steps farther down is the...*

🔟 **Intersection of Unter den Linden and Friedrichstrasse:** This is perhaps the most central crossroads in Berlin. And for several years more, it will be a mess as Berlin builds a new connection in its already extensive subway system. All over Berlin, you'll see big, colorful **water pipes** running aboveground. Wherever there are large construction projects, streets are laced with these drainage pipes. Berlin's high water table means that any new basement comes with lots of pumping out.

Looking at the jaunty DDR-style pedestrian lights at this intersection is a reminder that very little of the old East survives. Construction has been a theme since the Wall came down. The West lost no time in consuming the East; consequently, some have felt a wave of *Ost*-algia for the old days of East Berlin. At election time, a surprising number of formerly East Berlin voters still opt for the extreme left party, which has ties to the bygone Communist Party—although the East-West divide is no longer at the forefront of most voters' minds.

One symbol of that communist era has been given a reprieve: the DDR-style pedestrian lights you'll see along Unter den Lin-

den (and throughout much of the former East Berlin). The perky red and green men—called *Ampelmännchen*—were recently threatened with replacement by ordinary signs. But, after a 10-year court battle, the wildly popular DDR signals were kept after all.

When the little green *Ampelmännchen* says you can go, cross the construction zone that has taken over this stretch of Unter den Linden, and note the Ampelmann souvenir store across the street.

Before continuing down Unter den Linden, look farther down **Friedrichstrasse.** Before the war, this zone was the heart of Berlin. In the 1920s, Berlin was famous for its anything-goes love of life. This was the cabaret drag, a springboard to stardom for young and vampy entertainers like Marlene Dietrich. (Born in 1901, Dietrich starred in the first major German talkie—*The Blue Angel*—and then headed straight to Hollywood.)

Now Friedrichstrasse is lined with super-department stores and big-time hotels. Consider detouring to the megastore **Galeries Lafayette** (Mon-Sat 10:00-20:00, closed Sun); check out the vertical garden on its front wall, belly up to the amazing ground-floor viewpoint of its marble and glass waste-of-space interior, have lunch in its recommended basement food court, or, if the weather's nice, pick up some classy munchies here for a Gendarmenmarkt picnic. The short walk here provides some of Berlin's most jarring old-versus-new architectural contrasts—be sure to look up as you stroll. (If you were to continue down Friedrichstrasse from here, you'd wind up at Checkpoint Charlie in about 10 minutes.)

• *We've reached the end of Part 1 of this walk. This is a good place to take a break, if you wish, and pick up Part 2 another time. But if you're up for ambling on, head down Unter den Linden a few more blocks, past the large equestrian statue of Frederick the Great, then turn right into Bebelplatz.*

PART 2: BEBELPLATZ TO ALEXANDERPLATZ

• *Starting at Bebelplatz, head to the center of the square, and find the glass window in the pavement. We'll begin with some history and a spin tour.*

⑮ Bebelplatz

For centuries, up until the early 1700s, Prussia had been likened to a modern-day Sparta—it was all about its military. Voltaire famously said, "Whereas some states have an army, the Prussian army has a state." But Frederick the Great—who ruled from 1740 to 1786—established Prussia not just as a military power, but also as a cultural and intellectual heavyweight. This square was the center of the cultural capital that Frederick envisioned. His grand palace was just down the street.

Imagine that it's 1760. Pan around the square to see Frederick's contributions to Prussian culture. Everything is draped with Greek-inspired Prussian pomp. Sure, Prussia was a militaristic power. But Frederick also built an "Athens on the Spree"—an enlightened and cultured society.

To visually survey the square, start with the university across the street and spin counterclockwise:

🔟**Humboldt University,** across Unter den Linden, is one of Europe's greatest. Marx and Lenin (not the brothers or the sisters) studied here, as did the Grimms (both brothers) and more than two dozen Nobel Prize winners. Einstein, who was Jewish, taught here until taking a spot at Princeton in 1932 (smart guy). Used-book merchants set up their tables in front of the university.

Turn 90 degrees to the left to face the former **state library** (labeled *Juristische Fakultät*). Bombed in WWII, the library was rebuilt by the East German government in the original style only because Vladimir Lenin studied law here during much of his exile from Russia. If you climb to the second floor of the library and go through the door opposite the stairs, you'll see a 1968 vintage stained-glass window depicting Lenin's life's work with almost biblical reverence. On the ground floor is Tim's Espressobar, a great little café with light food, student prices, and garden seating (closed Sun, handy WC).

The far end of the square is closed off by one of Berlin's swankiest lodgings—**Hotel de Rome,** housed in a historic bank building with a spa and lap pool fitted into the former vault.

The round, Catholic **St. Hedwig's Church,** nicknamed the "upside-down teacup," is a statement of religious and cultural tolerance. The pragmatic Frederick the Great wanted to encourage the integration of Catholic Silesians after his empire annexed their region in 1742, and so the first Catholic church since the Reformation was built in Berlin. (St. Hedwig is the patron saint of Silesia, a region now shared by Germany, Poland, and the Czech Republic.) Like all Catholic churches in Berlin, St. Hedwig's is not on the street, but stuck in a kind of back lot—indicating inferiority to Protestant churches. You can step inside the church to see the cheesy DDR government renovation.

The ❶ **German State Opera** (Staatsoper) was bombed in 1941, rebuilt to bolster morale and to celebrate its centennial in 1943, and bombed again in 1945. It's currently undergoing an extensive renovation.

Now look down through the glass you're standing on: The room of empty bookshelves is a memorial repudiating a notorious Nazi **book burning** on this square. In 1933 staff and students from the university threw 20,000 newly forbidden books (authored by Einstein, Hemmingway, Freud, and T. S. Eliot, among others) into a huge bonfire on the orders of the Nazi propaganda minister, Joseph Goebbels. In fact, Goebbels himself tossed books onto the fire, condemning writers to the flames. He declared, "The era of extreme Jewish intellectualism has come to an end, and the German revolution has again opened the way for the true essence of being German."

The Prussian heritage of Frederick the Great was one of culture and enlightenment. Hitler chose this square to thoroughly squash those ideals, dramatically signaling that the era of tolerance and openness was over. Hitler was establishing a new age of intolerance where German-ness was correct and diversity was evil.

A plaque nearby reminds us of the prophetic quote by the German poet Heinrich Heine. In 1820, he wrote, "Where they burn books, in the end they will also burn people." The Nazis despised Heine because he was a Jew who converted to Christianity. A century later, his books were among those that went up in flames on this spot.

This monument reminds us of that chilling event in 1933, while also inspiring vigilance against the anti-intellectual scaremongers of today, who would burn the thoughts of people they fear to defend their culture from diversity.

• *Cross Unter den Linden to the university side. Just past the university is a Greek-temple-like building set in the small chestnut-tree-filled park.* *This is the...*

❶ Neue Wache (New Guardhouse)

The emperor's former guardhouse now holds the nation's main memorial to all "victims of war and tyranny." Look inside, where a replica of the Käthe Kollwitz statue, *Mother with Her Dead Son*, is enshrined in silence. It marks the tombs of Germany's unknown soldier and an unknown concentration camp victim. Read the powerful statement (posted in English left of entrance). The memorial, open to the sky, incorporates the elements—sunshine, rain, snow—falling on this modern-day *pietà*.

• *Next to the Neue Wache is Berlin's pink-yet-formidable Zeughaus (arsenal). Dating from 1695, it's considered the oldest building on the boulevard, and now houses the excellent* ⓲ *German History Museum—well worth a visit.*

Continue across a bridge to reach ⓴ *Museum Island (Museumsinsel), whose imposing Neoclassical buildings house some of Berlin's most impressive museums (including the Pergamon Museum—famous for its classical antiquities—and all worth the better part of a sightseeing day).*

For now, we'll check out a few other landmarks on the island. First is the big, inviting park called the...

㉑ Lustgarten

For 300 years, Museum Island's big central square has flip-flopped between being a military parade ground and a people-friendly park, depending upon the political tenor of the time. During the revolutions of 1848, the Kaiser's troops dispersed a protesting crowd that had assembled here, sending demonstrators onto footpaths. Karl Marx later commented, "It is impossible to have a revolution in a country where people stay off the grass."

Hitler enjoyed giving speeches from the top of the museum steps overlooking this square. In fact, he had the square landscaped to fit his symmetrical tastes and propaganda needs.

In 1999, the Lustgarten was made into a park (read the history posted in the corner opposite the church). On a sunny day, it's packed with people relaxing and is one of Berlin's most enjoyable public spaces.

• *The huge church next to the park is the...*

㉒ Berlin Cathedral (Berliner Dom)

This century-old church's bombastic Wilhelmian architecture is a Protestant assertion of strength. It seems to proclaim, "A mighty fortress is our God." The years of Kaiser Wilhelm's rule, from 1888 to 1918, were a busy age of building. Germany had recently been united (1871), and the emperor wanted to give his capital stature and legitimacy. Wilhelm's buildings are over-the-top statements: Neoclassical, Neo-Baroque, and Neo-Renais-

sance, with stucco and gold-tiled mosaics. This cathedral, while Protestant, is as ornate as if it were Catholic. With the emperor's lead, this ornate style came into vogue, and anyone who wanted to be associated with the royal class built this way. (Aside from the cathedral, the other big examples of Wilhelmian architecture in Berlin are the Reichstag—which we saw earlier—and the Kaiser Wilhelm Memorial Church.) The church is most impressive from the outside, and there's no way to even peek inside without a pricey ticket.

Inside, the great reformers (Luther, Calvin, and company) stand around the brilliantly restored dome like stern saints guarding their theology. Frederick I (Frederick the Great's gramps) rests in an ornate tomb (right transept, near entrance to dome). The 270-step climb to the outdoor dome gallery is tough but offers pleasant, breezy views of the city at the finish line. The crypt downstairs is not worth a look.

Cost and Hours: €7 includes access to dome gallery, not covered by Museum Island ticket, Mon-Sat 9:00-20:00, Sun 12:00-20:00, until 19:00 Oct-March, closes around 17:30 on concert days, interior closed but dome open during services, audioguide-€3, tel. 030/2026-9136, www.berliner-dom.de. The cathedral hosts many organ concerts (often on weekends, tickets at the door—prices range from free up to €50, but often around €10).

• *Kitty-corner across the main street from the Berlin Cathedral is a huge construction site, known as the...*

㉓ Humboldt-Forum Berliner Schloss

For centuries, this was the site of the Baroque palace of the Hohenzollern dynasty of Brandenburg and Prussia. Much of that palace actually survived World War II but was replaced by the communists with a blocky, Soviet-style "Palace" of the Republic—East Berlin's parliament building/entertainment complex and a showy symbol of the communist days. The landmark building fell into disrepair after reunification, and by 2009 had been dismantled.

After much debate about how to use this prime real estate, the German parliament decided to construct the Humboldt-Forum Berliner Schloss, a huge public venue filled with museums, shops, galleries, and concert halls behind a facade constructed in imitation of the original Hohenzollern palace. With a €600 million price tag, many Berliners consider the reconstruction plan

a complete waste of money. The latest news is that it should be finished by 2019.

In the meantime, the temporary, bright blue **Humboldt-Box** provides info and a viewing platform from which to survey the construction (until it gets in the way and also has to be demolished). Consider popping in for a look at the beautiful model, on the first floor up, showing this area as it was in 1900 (free, daily 10:00-19:00).

• *Head to the bridge just beyond the Berlin Cathedral, with views of the riverbank. Consider...*

Strolling and Cruising the Spree River

This river was once a symbol of division—the East German regime put nets underwater to stymie those desperate enough for freedom to swim to the West. With the reunification of Berlin, however, the Spree River has become people-friendly and welcoming. A park-like trail leads from the Berlin Cathedral to the Hauptbahnhof, with impromptu "beachside" beer gardens with imported sand, BBQs in pocket parks, and lots of locals walking their dogs, taking a lazy bike ride, or jogging.

You may notice "don't drop anchor" signs. There are still unexploded WWII bombs in Berlin, and many are in this river. Every month, several bombs are found at construction sites. Their triggers were set for the hard ground of Scottish testing grounds, and because Berlin sits upon soft soil, an estimated one of every ten bombs didn't explode.

The recommended ❷❹ **Spree River cruises** depart from the riverbank near the bridge by the Berlin Cathedral.

• *Before leaving the bridge, look upstream. In the distance, to the south, the pointy twin spires of the 13th-century Nikolai Church mark the center of medieval Berlin. This* **Nikolaiviertel** *(Viertel means "quarter") was restored by the DDR and became trendy in the last years of communism.*

Now look downstream: Farther off to the north is the gilded **New Synagogue** *dome, rebuilt after WWII bombing. Down at your feet, along the riverbank, you'll see the* ❷❺ **DDR Museum,** *with lots of hands-on exhibits and artifacts from everyday life in the former East Germany.*

Now continue walking straight toward the TV Tower, down the big boulevard, which here changes its name to...

Karl-Liebknecht-Strasse

The first big building on the left after the bridge is the **Radisson Blu Hotel** and shopping center, with a huge aquarium in the center. The elevator goes right through the middle of a deep-sea world. (You can see it from the unforgettable Radisson hotel lobby—tuck in your shirt and walk past the guards with the confidence of a guest who's sleeping there.) It's a huge glass cylinder rising high above the central bar (best seen from the left corner as you enter). Here in the center of the old communist capital, it seems that capitalism has settled in with a spirited vengeance.

In the park immediately across the street (a big jaywalk from the Radisson) are grandfatherly statues of **Marx** and **Engels** (nicknamed the "old pensioners"). Surrounding them are stainless-steel monoliths with evocative photos illustrating the struggles of the workers of the world.

Farther along, where Karl-Liebknecht-Strasse intersects with Spandauer Strasse, look right to see the red-brick **city hall**. It was built after the revolutions of 1848 and was arguably the first democratic building in the city.

Continue toward ❷❻ **Marien Church** (from 1270), with its spire mirroring the TV Tower. Inside, an artist's rendering helps you follow the interesting but very faded old "Dance of Death" mural that wraps around the narthex inside the door.

• *Immediately across the street from the church, detour a half-block down little Rosenstrasse to find a beautiful memorial set in a park.*

❷❼ **Women's Protest Memorial:** This is a reminder of a successful and courageous protest against Nazi policies. In 1943, when "privileged Jews" (men married to Gentile women) were arrested, their wives demonstrated en masse on this street, home to Berlin's oldest synagogue (now gone). They actually won the freedom of their men. Note the Berliner on the bench nearby. As most Berliners did, he looks the other way, even when these courageous women demonstrated that you could speak up and be heard under the Nazis.

• *Back on Karl-Liebknecht-Strasse, look up at the 1,200-foot-tall...*

❷❽ **TV Tower (Fernsehturm):** Built (with Swedish know-how) in 1969 for the 20th anniversary of the communist government, the

tower was meant to show the power of the atheistic state at a time when DDR leaders were having the crosses removed from church domes and spires. But when the sun hit the tower—the greatest spire in East Berlin—a huge cross was reflected on the mirrored ball. Cynics called it "God's Revenge." East Berliners dubbed the tower the "Tele-Asparagus." They joked that if it fell over, they'd have an elevator to the West.

The tower has a fine view from halfway up, offering a handy city orientation and an interesting look at the flat, red-roofed sprawl of Berlin—including a peek inside the city's many courtyards (€13, daily until 24:00). The retro tower is quite trendy these days, so it can be crowded (your ticket comes with an assigned entry time). Consider a kitschy trip to the observation deck for the view and lunch in its revolving restaurant (mediocre food,

BERLIN

€12 plates, horrible lounge music, reservations smart for dinner, tel. 030/242-3333, www.tv-turm.de).

• *Walk four more minutes down the boulevard past the TV Tower and toward the big railway overpass. Just before the bridge, on the left, is the half-price ticket booth called* **Hekticket**—*stop in to see what's on.*

Walk under the train bridge and continue for a long half-block (passing the Galeria Kaufhof mall). Turn right onto a broad pedestrian street, and go through the low tunnel into the big square where blue U-Bahn station signs mark...

㉙ Alexanderplatz

This square was the commercial pride and joy of East Berlin. The Kaufhof department store (now Galeria Kaufhof) was the ultimate shopping mecca for Easterners. It, along with the two big surviving 1920s "functionalist" buildings, defined the square. Alexanderplatz is still a landmark, with a major U-Bahn/S-Bahn station. The once-futuristic, now-retro "World Time Clock," installed in 1969, is a nostalgic favorite and remains a popular meeting point.

Stop in the square for a coffee and to people-watch. You may see the dueling human hot-dog stands. These hot-dog hawkers wear ingenious harnesses that let them cook and sell tasty, cheap German sausages on the fly. (Grillwalker is the original company; Grillrunner is the copycat.) While the square can get a little rough at night, it's generally a great scene.

• *Our orientation stroll is finished. From here, you can hike back a bit to catch the riverboat tour or visit Museum Island or the German History museums, take in the sights south of Unter den Linden, venture into the colorful Prenzlauer Berg neighborhood, or consider extending this foray into eastern Berlin by way of Karl-Marx-Allee. These options are covered in detail in the next section.*

Sights in Eastern Berlin

NEAR THE BRANDENBURG GATE

Many of Berlin's top sights and landmarks in this area are described in detail in the self-guided walk above (including the **Brandenburg Gate**, the **Memorial to the Murdered Jews of Europe**, **Pariser Platz**, and **Unter den Linden.**

▲▲▲Reichstag

Germany's historic parliament building—completed in 1894,

burned in 1933, sad and lonely in a no-man's land throughout the Cold War, and finally rebuilt and topped with a glittering glass

 cupola in 1999—is a symbol of a proudly reunited nation. It's fascinating to climb up the twin ramps that spiral through its dome. Because of security concerns, getting in requires a reservation.

BERLIN

Cost and Hours: Free, but reservations required—see below, daily 8:00-24:00, last entry at 22:00, metal detectors, no big luggage allowed, Platz der Republik 1; S- or U-Bahn: Friedrichstrasse, Brandenburger Tor, or Bundestag; tel. 030/2273-2152, www.bundestag.de.

Reservations: To visit the dome, you'll need to **reserve online;** spots often book up several days in advance. Go to www.bundestag.de, and from the "Visit the Bundestag" menu, select "Online registration." After choosing your preferred date and time, you'll be sent an email link to a website where you'll enter details for each person in your party. A final email will contain your reservation (with a letter you must print out and bring with you).

If you're in Berlin without a reservation, try dropping by the tiny visitors center on the Tiergarten side of Scheidemannstrasse, across from Platz der Republik, to see if any tickets are available (open daily 8:00-20:00, until 18:00 Nov-March; go early to avoid lines; you must book no less than 2 hours and no more than 2 days out; when booking, the whole party must be present and ID is required).

Another option for visiting the dome, though a bit pricey, is to make lunch or dinner reservations for the rooftop restaurant, Käfer Dachgarten (€22-25 lunches, €30-34 dinners, daily 9:00-16:30 & 18:30-24:00, last access at 22:00, reserve well in advance at tel. 030/2262-9933 or www.feinkost-kaefer.de/berlin).

Getting In: Report a few minutes before your appointed time to the temporary-looking entrance facility in front of the Reichstag, and be ready to show ID and your reservation print-out. After passing through a security check, you'll wait with other visitors for a guard to take you to the Reichstag entrance.

Tours: Pick up the English *Outlooks* **flier** when you exit the elevator at the top of the Reichstag. The free **audioguide** explains the building and narrates the view as you wind up the spiral ramp to the top of the dome; the commentary starts automatically as you step onto the bottom of the ramp.

◉ Self-Guided Tour: The open, airy lobby towers 100 feet high, with 65-foot-tall colors of the German flag. See-through glass doors show the **central legislative chamber.** The message:

BERLIN

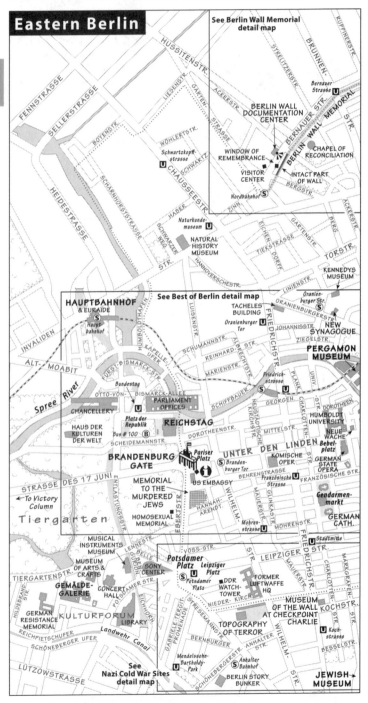

Eastern Berlin

See Berlin Wall Memorial detail map

FENNSTRASSE
SELLERSTRASSE
HEIDESTRASSE
INVALIDEN
ALT- MOABIT
BOYENSTR.
SCHARNHORSTSTRASSE
SCHWARTZKOPFF-strasse
CHAUSSEESTR.
HUSSITENSTR.
LIESENSTR.
GARTENSTR.
ACKERSTR.
STRASSE
WÖHLERTSTR.
SCHWARTZ
SCHWARZER WEG
HABER
Naturkunde-museum
STRELITZERSTR.
BRUNNEN-STR.
Bernauer Strasse U
BERLIN WALL MEMORIAL
BERLIN WALL DOCUMENTATION CENTER
CHAPEL OF RECONCILIATION
WINDOW OF REMEMBRANCE
VISITOR CENTER
INTACT PART OF WALL
Nordbahnhof S
BERGSTR.
ZINN
BERNAUER STR.
BERG-STR.
ACKERSTR.

NATURAL HISTORY MUSEUM
EICHEN-DORF
TIEKSTRASSE
GARTENSTR.
TORSTR.
HANNOVERSCHESTR.
LINIENSTR.

KENNEDYS MUSEUM

HAUPTBAHNHOF & EURAIDE S
Haupt-bahnhof S
See Best of Berlin detail map
TACHELES BUILDING
Oranienburger Str. S
Oranien-burger Str.
ORANIENBURGERSTR.
JOHANNISSTR.
ZIEGELSTR.
FRIEDRICHSTR.
NEW SYNAGOGUE
PERGAMON MUSEUM

HUMBOLDTHAFEN
FÜRST-BISMARCK-STR.
KAPELLE-UFER
LUISENSTR.
SCHUMANNSTR.
REINHARDTSTR.
MARIENSTR.
ALDRECHT STR.
SCHIFFBAUER
PLANK
GEORGEN
UNIV.
CHARLOTTEN-STR.
DOROTHEEN-STR.

Spree River
OTTO-VON-BISMARCK-ALLEE
Bundestag U
CHANCELLERY
PARLIAMENT OFFICES
Friedrich-strasse S
NEUSTÄDTISCHE
KIRCHSTR.
MITTELSTR.
HUMBOLDT UNIVERSITY
NEUE WACHE
Bebel-platz

HAUS DER KULTUREN DER WELT
Platz der Republik
Bus # 100 B
SCHEIDEMANNSTR.
REICHSTAG
DOROTHEENSTR.
UNTER DEN LINDEN
KOMISCHE OPER
GERMAN STATE OPERA
FRANZÖSISCHE STR.

STRASSE DES 17 JUNI
ENTLASTUNGSSTR.
Pariser Platz
BRANDENBURG GATE
Branden-burger Tor S
MEMORIAL TO THE MURDERED JEWS
US EMBASSY
BEHRENSTRASSE
Französische Strasse U
GLINKASTR.
MAUERSTR.
GENDARMEN-markt
GERMAN CATH.

To Victory Column ←
Tiergarten
HOMOSEXUAL MEMORIAL
EBERTSTR.
HANNAH-ARENDT-
WILHELM
Mohren-strasse U
MOHRENSTR.
FRIEDRICHSTR.
Stadtmitte U

MUSICAL INSTRUMENTS MUSEUM
MUSEUM OF ARTS & CRAFTS
LENNÉSTR.
VOSS-STR.
BELLE
GÖRING
Potsdamer Platz U
Leipziger Platz
Potsdamer Platz S
LEIPZIGER STR.
KAUERSTR.
CHARLOTTEN-STR.
MARKGRAFEN-STR.

GEMÄLDE-GALERIE
SONY CENTER
CONCERT HALL
KULTURFORUM
LIBRARY
EICHHORN
DDR WATCH-TOWER
FORMER LUFTWAFFE HQ
STRESEMANNSTR.
NIEDER-KIRCH-
MUSEUM OF THE WALL AT CHECKPOINT CHARLIE
KOCHSTR.
Koch-strasse U

TIERGARTENSTR.
HILDEBRAND-STR.
GERMAN RESISTANCE MEMORIAL
REICHPIETSCHUFER
SCHÖNEBERGER UFER
Landwehr Canal
GABRIELE-TERGIT-PROMENADE
BERNBURGER STR.
TOPOGRAPHY OF TERROR
ANHALTER STR.
WILHELM
BESSELSTR.

LÜTZOWSTRASSE
See Nazi Cold War Sites detail map
Mendelssohn-Bartholdy-Park
Anhalter Bahnhof S
BERLIN STORY BUNKER
SCHÖNEBERGER STR.
JEWISH MUSEUM →

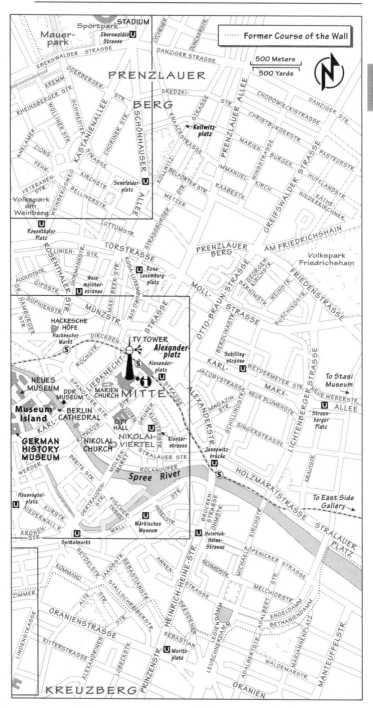

...... Former Course of the Wall

500 Meters
500 Yards

N

Mauer-
park
Sportpark
STADIUM
Eberswalder
Strasse

PRENZLAUER
BERG

EBERSWALDER STRASSE
KREM
ODERBERGER STR.
RHEINSBERGER STR.
SCHWEDTER STRASSE
KASTANIENALLEE
CHORINER STR.
SCHÖNHAUSER ALLEE
ANKLAMER
ZIONS-
FEHR-
VETERANEN- STR.
KIRCHSTR.
RHEINSBERGSWEG
BELLINSTR.
Volkspark
am
Weinberg
Rosenthaler
Platz
LINIEN-
ROSENTHALER STR.
GIPSSTR.
AUGUSTSTR.
GORMANNSTR.
SOPHIENSTR.
HAMBURGER STR.
HACKESCHE
HÖFE
Hackescher
Markt
NEUES
MUSEUM
Museum
Island
GERMAN
HISTORY
MUSEUM
WERDER.
Hausvogtei-
platz
KURSTR.
NIEDERWALL R.
KRONEN-
STR.
Spittelmarkt
ZIMMER.
LINDENSTRASSE
KOMMAND.
ORANIENSTRASSE
RITTERSTRASSE
SEYDELSTR.
JAKOBSTR.
ALTE STR.
STALLSCHREIBERSTR.
SEBASTIANSTR.
ANNEN-
PRINZENSTR.
ALEXANDRINEN
LÜBECKER STR.
Moritz-
platz
SEBASTIAN
KREUZBERG
ORANIEN
HEINRICH-HEINE-STR.
DRESDENER STR.
LEGIENDAMM
SCHMIDSTR.
MICHAEL
KÖPENICKER STRASSE
ADALBERTSTR.
KIRCHSTR.
MELCHIORSTR.
ENGELDAMM
BETHANIENDAMM
MARIANNENPLATZ
ADALBERTSTR.
LEUSCHNERDAMM
WALDEMARSTR.
MANTEUFFELSTR.
Heinrich-
Heine-
Strasse
Märkisches
Museum
WALL
FISCHER-
INSEL
INGELSTR.
ROLANDUFER
STRALAUER STR.
Spree River
GERTRAUDEN-
STR.
BRÜCKEN-
STRASSE
OLIM STK.
HOLZMARKTSTRASSE
STRALAUER
PLATZ
To East Side
Gallery
KRAUTSTR.
Jannowitz-
brücke
Klosterstrasse
NIKOLAI-
VIERTEL
CITY
HALL
NIKOLAI
CHURCH
BREITE STR.
MOLKEN-
MARKT
GRUNER
LIEBKNECHT
SPANDAUER STR.
MARIEN
CHURCH
DDR
MUSEUM
BERLIN
CATHEDRAL
KARL-
TV TOWER
MITTE
Alexander-
platz
Alexander-
platz
ALEXANDERSTR.
SINGERSTRASSE
Straus-
berger
Platz
ALLEE
To Stasi
Museum
NEUE WEBERSTR.
LICHTENBERGER STRASSE
MARX-
KARL-
Schilling-
strasse
WEYDEMEYER STR.
JACOBYSTRASSE
SCHILLINGSTR.
NEUE BLUMENSTR.
MAGAZIN-
STR.
BERLOINARSTR.
BÜSCHINGSTR.
Schilling-
strasse
FRIEDENSTRASSE
Volkspark
Friedrichshain
AM FRIEDRICHSHAIN
GREIFSWALDER STRASSE
KÄTHE-
NIEDERKIRCHNER
HUFELANDSTR.
PASTEURSTR.
MARIEN-
BURGER
IMMANUEL-
KIRCH
RAABESTR.
METZER
BELFORTER STR.
KOLLWITZ
Senefelder-
platz
Rosa-
Luxemburg-
platz
Wein-
meister-
strasse
TORSTRASSE
MÜNZSTR.
DIRCKSEN-
ROCHSTR.
STRASSE
MAX-
BEER-STR.
ROSA-LUXEMBURG STR.
PRENZLAUER
BERG
MOLL-
STRASSE
OTTO-BRAUN-STRASSE
GEORGEN-
KIRCHSTR.
BERNIMSTR.
WEINSTR.
Kollwitz-
platz
SREDZKI-
STR.
STRASSE
KNAACKSTRASSE
KOLLWITZ STRASSE
STRASSBURGERSTR.
LOTTUMSTR.
DANZIGER STRASSE
CHODOWIECKISTRASSE
CHRISTBURGERSTR.
DANZIGER STR.
WINSSTR.
PRENZLAUER ALLEE
DUNCKERSTR.
LYCHENER
SCHÖNHAUSER ALLEE

There will be no secrets in this government. Look inside. Spreading his wings behind the podium is a stylized German eagle, the *Bundestagsadler* (a.k.a. the "fat hen"), representing the Bundestag (each branch of government has its own symbolic eagle). Notice the doors marked *Ja* (Yes), *Nein* (No), and *Enthalten* (Abstain)... an homage to the Bundestag's traditional "sheep jump" way of counting votes by exiting the chamber through the corresponding door (for critical votes, however, all 631 members vote with electronic cards).

Ride the elevator to the base of the glass **dome.** Pick up the free audioguide and take some time to study the photos and read the circle of captions (around the base of the central funnel) for an excellent exhibit telling the Reichstag story. Then study the surrounding architecture: a broken collage of new on old, torn between antiquity and modernity, like Germany's history. Notice the dome's giant and unobtrusive sunscreen that moves as necessary with the sun. Peer down through the skylight to look over the shoulders of the elected representatives at work. For Germans, the best view from here is down—keeping a close eye on their government.

Start at the ramp nearest the elevator and wind up to the top of the **double ramp.** Take a 360-degree survey of the city as you hike: The big park is the **Tiergarten,** the "green lungs of Berlin." Beyond that is the **Teufelsberg** ("Devil's Hill"). Built of rubble from the destroyed city in the late 1940s, it was famous during the Cold War as a powerful ear of the West—notice the telecommunications tower on top. Knowing the bombed-out and bulldozed story of their city, locals say, "You have to be suspicious when you see the nice, green park."

Find the **Victory Column** (Siegessäule), glimmering in the middle of the park. Hitler moved it in the 1930s from in front of the Reichstag to its present position in the Tiergarten as part of his grandiose vision for postwar Berlin. Next, scenes of the new Berlin spiral into view—**Potsdamer Platz,** marked by the conical glass tower that houses Sony's European headquarters. Continue circling left, and find the green chariot atop the **Brandenburg Gate.** Just to its left is the curving fish-like roof of the **DZ Bank** building, designed by the unconventional American architect Frank Gehry. The **Memorial to the Murdered Jews of Europe** stretches south of the Brandenburg Gate. Next, you'll see **former**

BERLIN

East Berlin and the city's next huge construction zone, with a forest of 300-foot-tall skyscrapers in the works. Notice the **TV Tower,** the **Berlin Cathedral's** massive dome, and the golden dome of the **New Synagogue.**

Follow the train tracks in the distance to the left toward Berlin's huge main train station, the **Hauptbahnhof.** Complete your spin-tour with the blocky, postmodern **Chancellery,** the federal government's headquarters. Continue spiraling up. You'll come across all the same sights again, twice, from a higher vantage point.

ON OR NEAR MUSEUM ISLAND (MUSEUMSINSEL)

Three Museum Island landmarks—the **Lustgarten, Berlin Cathedral,** and the **Humboldt-Box**—are described earlier, in my "Best of Berlin Walk."

The Museums of Museum Island

Five of Berlin's top museums are concentrated on this aptly named, centrally located island, just up Unter den Linden from the Brandenburg Gate. (They're all part of the Staatliche Museen zu Berlin.) The earliest building—the Altes Museum—went up in the 1820s, and the rest of the complex began taking shape in the 1840s under King Friedrich Wilhelm IV, who envisioned the island as an oasis of culture and learning.

A formidable renovation is under way on Museum Island. When complete (it's hoped in 2019), a new visitors center—the James-Simon-Galerie—will link the Pergamon Museum with the Altes Museum, the Pergamon will get a fourth wing, tunnels will lace the complex together, and this will become one of the grandest museum zones in Europe. In the meantime, pardon their dust.

Cost: The €18 Museum Island Pass combo-ticket—covering all five museums—is a far better value than buying individual entries, which range from €10 to €14. All five museums are also included in the city's €24 Museum Pass Berlin. Special exhibits are extra.

Hours: Museum hours are 10:00-18:00 (until 20:00 on Thu). The Pergamon and Neues museums are open daily; the Old National Gallery, Bode Museum, and Altes Museum are open Tue-Sun, closed Mon.

When to Go: Mornings are busiest, and you're likely to find long lines any time of day on Saturday or Sunday. The least-crowded time is Thursday evening, when the museums are open

BERLIN

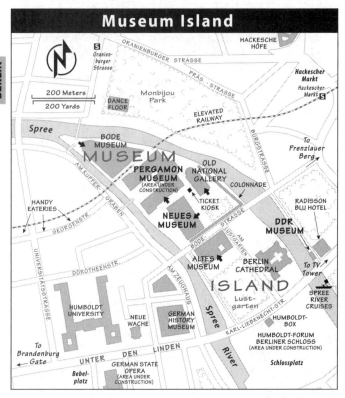

Museum Island

late. Only the Pergamon Museum tends to have serious lines, though.

Crowd-Beating Tips: Avoid the lines for the Pergamon Museum by purchasing a timed ticket online, or book a free timed-entry reservation if you have a Museum Pass Berlin or a Museum Island Pass (www.smb.museum). Both passes allow you to skip ticket-buying lines at the other museums on the island, but online booking is your only option for getting right to the head of the Pergamon's line.

Getting There: The nearest S-Bahn station is Hackescher Markt, about a 10-minute walk away. From hotels in Prenzlauer Berg, ride tram #M-1 to the end of line, and you're right at the Pergamon Museum.

Information: Tel. 030/266-424-242, www.smb.museum.

Eating: For lunch in the neighborhood, follow the elevated train tracks away from the Pergamon down Georgenstrasse, or cross the Friedrichsbrücke bridge and follow signs for five minutes to Hackescher Markt, with its multitude of eateries.

Just for Fun: Germany's formidable leader, Angela Merkel, could live in the expansive digs at the Chancellery. But she and her husband (who's a professor right here at Humboldt University) have long lived in an apartment overlooking Museum Island. You'll see a couple of policemen providing modest protection in front of her place on Am Kupfergraben, directly across the bridge from the Pergamon Museum.

▲▲▲Pergamon Museum (Pergamonmuseum)

The star attraction of this world-class museum, part of Berlin's Collection of Classical Antiquities (Antikensammlung), is the

fantastic and gigantic Pergamon Altar...which is off-limits to visitors until 2019, as the museum undergoes major renovation. But there's much more to see here, including the Babylonian Ishtar Gate (slathered with glazed blue tiles from the sixth century B.C.) and ancient Mesopotamian, Roman, and early

Islamic treasures. During the renovation, some of the museum's Greek and Roman pieces are temporarily installed at the Altes Museum (but Hellenistic architecture and artworks won't be seen again until 2019).

Visting the Museum: Make ample use of the superb audioguide (included with admission)—it will broaden your experience.

From the entry hall, head up the stairs and all the way back to 575 B.C., to the Fertile Crescent—Mesopotamia (today's Iraq). The Assyrian ruler Nebuchad-

nezzar II, who amassed a vast empire and enormous wealth, wanted to build a suitably impressive processional entryway to his capital city, Babylon, to honor the goddess Ishtar. His creation, the blue **Ishtar Gate,** inspired awe and obedience in anyone who came to his city. This is a reconstruction, using some original components. The gate itself is embellished with two animals: a bull and a mythical dragon-like combination of lion, cobra, eagle, and scorpion. The long hall leading to the main gate—designed for a huge processional of deities to celebrate the new year—is decorated with a chain of blue and yellow glazed tiles with 120 strolling lions (representing the goddess Ishtar). To get the big picture, find the model of the original site in the center of the hall.

Pass through the gate, and flash-forward 700 years to the

ancient Roman city of Miletus. Dominating this room is the 95-foot-wide, 55-foot-high **Market Gate of Miletus,** destroyed

by an earthquake centuries ago and now painstakingly reconstructed here in Berlin. The exquisite mosaic floor from a Roman villa in Miletus has two parts: In the square panel, the musician Orpheus strokes his lyre to charm the animals; in stark contrast, in the nearby rectangular mosaic (from an adjacent room), hunters pursue wild animals.

These main exhibits are surrounded by smaller galleries. Upstairs is the **Museum of Islamic Art.** It contains fine carpets, tile work, the Aleppo Room (with ornately painted wooden walls from an early 17th-century home in today's Syria; since it was commissioned by a Christian, it incorporates Arabic, Persian, and

biblical themes), and the Mshatta Facade (walls and towers from one of the early eighth-century Umayyad "desert castles," from today's Jordan).

▲▲Neues (New) Museum

Oddly, Museum Island's so-called "new" museum features the oldest stuff around. There are three collections here: the Egyptian Collection (with the famous bust of Queen Nefertiti), the Museum of Prehistory and Early History, and some items from the Collection of Classical Antiquities (artifacts from ancient Troy—famously excavated by German adventurer Heinrich Schliemann—and Cyprus).

After being damaged in World War II and sitting in ruins for some 40 years, the Neues Museum has been gorgeously rebuilt. Everything is well-described by posted English information and the fine audioguide (included with admission), which celebrates new knowledge about ancient Egyptian civilization and offers fascinating insights into workaday Egyptian life as it describes the vivid papyrus collection, slice-of-life artifacts, and dreamy wax portraits decorating mummy cases (for more on the museum, see www.neues-museum.de).

Visiting the Museum: Pick up a floor plan showing the suggested route, then head up the central staircase.

The top draw here is the Egyptian art—clearly one of the

BERLIN

world's best collections. But let's face it: The main reason to visit is to enjoy one of the great thrills in art appreciation—gazing into the still young and beautiful face of Queen Nefertiti. If you're in a pinch for time, make a beeline to her (floor 2, far corner of Egyptian Collection in Room 210).

To tour the whole collection, start at the top (floor 3), which is where you'll find the **prehistory section.** The entire floor is filled with Stone Age, Ice Age, and Bronze Age items. You'll see early human remains, tools, spearheads, and pottery.

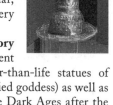

The most interesting item on this floor (in corner Room 305) is the tall, conehead-like **Golden Hat,** made of paper-thin hammered gold leaf. Created by an early Celtic civilization in Central Europe, it's particularly exquisite for something so old (from the Bronze Age, around 1000 B.C.). The circles on the hat represent the sun, moon, and other celestial bodies—leading archaeologists to believe that this headwear could double as a calendar, showing how the sun and moon sync up every 19 years.

Down on floor 2, you'll find **early history** exhibits on migrations, barbarians, and ancient

Rome (including larger-than-life statues of Helios and an unidentified goddess) as well as a fascinating look at the Dark Ages after the fall of Rome.

Still on floor 2, cross to the other side of the building for the **Egyptian** section. On the way, you'll pass through the impressive Papyrus Collection—a large room of seemingly empty glass cases. Press a button to watch a 3,000-year-old piece of primitive "paper" (made of aquatic reeds), imprinted with primitive text, trundle out of its protective home.

Then, finally, in a room all her own, is the 3,000-year-old bust of **Queen Nefertiti** (the wife of King Akhenaton, c. 1340 B.C.)—the most famous piece of Egyptian art in Europe. (Note that she's had it with the paparazzi—photos of her are strictly *verboten*.) Called "Berlin's most beautiful woman,"

Nefertiti has all the right beauty marks: long neck, symmetrical face, and the perfect amount of makeup. And yet, she's not completely idealized. Notice the fine wrinkles that show she's human (though these only enhance her beauty). Like a movie star discreetly sipping a glass of wine at a sidewalk café, Nefertiti seems somehow more dignified in person. The bust never left its studio, but served as a master model for all other portraits of the queen. (That's probably why the left eye was never inlaid.) Stare at her long enough, and you may get the sensation that she's winking at you. Hey, beautiful!

How the queen arrived in Germany is a tale out of *Indiana Jones*. The German archaeologist Ludwig Borchardt uncovered her in the Egyptian desert in 1912. The Egyptian Department of Antiquities had first pick of all the artifacts uncovered on their territory. After the first takings, they divided the rest 50/50 with the excavators. When Borchardt presented Nefertiti to the Egyptians, they passed her over, never bothering to examine her closely. Unsubstantiated rumors persist that Borchardt misled the Egyptians in order to keep the bust for himself—rumors that have prompted some Egyptians to call for the return of Nefertiti (just as the Greeks are lobbying the British to return the Parthenon frieze currently housed in the British Museum). Although this bust is not particularly representative of Egyptian art in general—and despite increasing claims that her long neck suggests she's a Neoclassical fake—Nefertiti has become a symbol of Egyptian art by popular acclaim.

The Egyptian Collection continues with other sculptures, including kneeling figures holding inscribed stone tablets. You'll also see entire walls from tombs and (in the basement—floor 0) a sea of large sarcophagi.

▲Old National Gallery (Alte Nationalgalerie)

This gallery, behind the Neues Museum and Altes Museum, is designed to look like a Greek temple. Spanning three floors, it focuses on art (mostly paintings) from the 19th century: Romantic German paintings (which I find most interesting) on the top floor, and French and German Impressionists and German Realists on the first and second floors. You likely won't recognize any specific paintings, but it's still an enjoyable stroll through German culture from the century in which that notion first came to mean something. The included audioguide explains the highlights.

Visiting the Museum: Start on the third floor, with Romantic canvases and art of the Goethe era (roughly 1770-1830), and work your way down. Use the audioguide to really delve into these romanticized, vivid looks at life in Germany in the 19th century and before. As you stroll through the Romantic paintings—the museum's strength—keep in mind that they were created about the time (mid-late 19th century) that Germans were first working toward a single, unified nation. By glorifying pristine German landscapes and a rugged, virtuous people, these painters evoked the region's high-water mark—the Middle Ages, when "Germany" was a patchwork of powerful and wealthy merchant city-states. Linger over dreamy townscapes with Gothic cathedrals and castles that celebrate medieval Ger-

man might. Still lifes, genre paintings of everyday scenes (often with subtle social commentary), and portraits ranging from idealized tow-headed children to influential German leaders (such as Otto von Bismarck, pictured) strum the heartstrings of anyone with Teutonic blood. The Düsseldorf School excelled at Romantic landscapes (such as Carl Friedrich Lessing's *Knight's Castle*). Some of these canvases nearly resemble present-

day fantasy paintings. Perhaps the best-known artist in the collection is Caspar David Friedrich, who specialized in dramatic scenes celebrating grandeur and the solitary hero. His *The Monk by the Sea (Der Mönch am Meer)* shows a lone figure standing on a sand dune, pondering a vast, turbulent expanse of sea and sky.

On the second floor, you'll find one big room of minor works by bigger-name French artists, including Renoir, Cézanne, Manet, Monet, and Rodin. Another room is devoted to the Romantic Hans von Marées, the influential early Symbolist Arnold Böcklin, and other artists of the "German Roman" (Deutschrömer) movement—Germans who lived in, and were greatly influenced by,

Rome. Artists of the Munich School are represented by naturalistic canvases of landscapes or slice-of-life scenes.

On the first floor, 19th-century Realism reigns. While the Realist Adolph Menzel made his name painting elegant royal gatherings and historical events, his *Iron Rolling Mill (Das Eisenwalzwerk)* captures the gritty side of his moment in history—the emergence of the Industrial Age—with a warts-and-all look at steelworkers toiling in a hellish factory. The first floor also hosts a sculpture collection, with works by great sculptors both foreign (the Italian Canova, the Dane Thorvaldsen) and German (Johann Gottfried Schadow's delightful *Die Prinzessinnen,* showing the dynamic duo of Prussian princesses, Louise and Frederike). Also on the first floor, near the sculptures, look for a low-key room left unrestored so visitors can recall the days when the DDR ran this museum.

Bode Museum
At the "prow" of Museum Island, the Bode Museum (designed to appear as if it's rising up from the river) is worth a brief stop. Just inside, a grand statue of Frederick William of Brandenburg on horseback, curly locks blowing in the wind, welcomes you into the lonely halls of the museum. This fine building contains a hodge-podge of collections: Byzantine art, historic coins, ecclesiastical art, sculptures, and medals commemorating the fall of the Berlin Wall and German reunification. For a free, quick look at its lavish interior, climb the grand staircase to the charming café on the first floor.

Altes (Old) Museum
Perhaps the least interesting of the five museums, this building features the rest of the Collection of Classical Antiquities—namely, Etruscan, Roman, and Greek art. It also contains Greek and Roman sculptures, vases, and some bronze figurines from the currently closed north wing of the Pergamon Museum.

Near Museum Island
The German History Museum is on Unter den Linden just before the boulevard crosses to Museum Island; the Palace of Tears is north of the boulevard, very near the Spree River. The DDR Museum sits on the other side of Museum Island, on the riverbank directly across from the Berlin Cathedral.

▲▲▲German History Museum
(Deutsches Historisches Museum)
This fantastic museum is a two-part affair: the pink former Prussian arsenal building and the I. M. Pei-designed annex. The main building (fronting Unter den Linden) houses the permanent col-

lection, offering the best look at German history under one roof, anywhere. The modern annex features good temporary exhibits surrounded by the work of a great contemporary architect. While this city has more than its share of hokey "museums" that slap together WWII and Cold War bric-a-brac, then charge too much for admission, this thoughtfully presented museum—with more than 8,000 artifacts telling not just the story of Berlin, but of all Germany—is clearly the top history museum in town. If you need a break during your visit, there's a restful café with terrace seating in season.

Cost and Hours: €8, daily 10:00-18:00, Unter den Linden 2, tel. 030/2030-4751, www.dhm.de. For the most informative visit, invest in the excellent €3 audioguide, with six hours of info to choose from.

Getting In: If the ticket-buying line is long at the main entrance, try circling around the back to the Pei annex (to reach it, head down the street to the left of the museum—called Hinter dem Giesshaus), where entry lines are usually shorter (but audioguides for the permanent exhibit are available only at the main desk).

Visiting the Museum: The permanent collection packs two huge rectangular floors of the old arsenal building with historical objects, photographs, and models—all well-described in English and intermingled with multimedia stations to help put everything in context. From the lobby, head upstairs to the **first floor** and work your way chronologically down. This floor traces German history from A.D. 500 to 1918, with exhibits on early cultures, the Middle Ages, Reformation, Thirty Years' War, German Empire, and World War I. You'll see lots of models of higgledy-piggledy medieval towns and castles, tapestries, suits of armor, busts of great Germans, a Turkish tent from the Ottoman siege of Vienna (1683), flags from German unification in 1871 (the first time "Germany" existed as a nation), exhibits on everyday life in the tenements of the Industrial Revolution, and much more.

History marches on through the 20th century on the **ground floor,** including the Weimar Republic, Nazism, World War II, Allied occupation, and a divided Germany. Propaganda posters trumpet Germany's would-be post-WWI savior, Adolf Hitler. Look for the model of the impossibly huge, 950-foot-high, 180,000-capacity domed hall Hitler wanted to erect in the heart of Berlin, which he planned to re-envision as Welthauptstadt Germania, the "world capital" of his far-reaching Third Reich. Another model shows the nauseating reality of Hitler's grandiosity: a crematorium at Auschwitz-Birkenau concentration camp in occupied Poland. The exhibit wraps up with chunks of the Berlin Wall, reunification, and a quick look at Germany today.

For architecture buffs, the big attraction is the **Pei annex** behind the history museum, which complements the museum with often-fascinating temporary exhibits. From the old building, cross through the courtyard (with the Pei glass canopy overhead) to reach the annex. A striking glassed-in spiral staircase unites four floors with surprising views and lots of light. It's here that you'll experience why Pei—famous for his glass pyramid at Paris' Louvre—is called the "perfector of classical modernism," "master of light," and a magician at uniting historical buildings with new ones.

▲Palace of Tears (Tränenpalast) at Friedrichstrasse Station

The border station attached to Friedrichstrasse train station was where Westerners visiting loved ones in the East would be checked before crossing back into the free world. The scene of so many sad farewells, it earned the nickname "Tränenpalast" (palace of tears). It finally closed in 1990, but the 1962 building survives. An exhibit shows everyday life in a divided Germany, with a fascinating peek into the paranoid border-control world of the DDR.

Cost and Hours: Free, includes excellent audioguide, Tue-Fri 9:00-19:00, Sat-Sun 10:00-18:00, closed Mon, on the river side of the Friedrichstrasse station, Reichstagufer 17, tel. 030/4677-7790, www.hdg.de/berlin.

▲▲DDR Museum

The exhibits here offer an interesting look at life in the former East Germany without the negative spin most museums give. It's well-stocked with kitschy everyday items from the communist period, plus photos, video clips, and concise English explanations. The exhibits are interactive—you're encouraged to pick up and handle anything that isn't behind glass.

Cost and Hours: €7, daily 10:00-20:00, Sat until 22:00, just across the Spree from Museum Island at Karl-Liebknecht-Strasse 1, tel. 030/847-123-731, www.ddr-museum.de.

Visiting the Museum: You'll crawl through a Trabant car (designed by East German engineers to compete with the West's popular VW Beetle) and pick up some DDR-era black humor ("East Germany had 39 newspapers, four radio stations, two TV channels...and one opinion"). The reconstructed communist-era home lets you tour the kitchen, living room, bedrooms, and more. You'll learn about the *dacha*—the simple countryside cottages (owned by one in six East Germans) used for weekend retreats from the grimy city. (Others vacationed on the Baltic Coast, where nudism was all the rage, as a very revealing display explains.) Lounge in DDR

cinema chairs as you view a subtitled propaganda film or cli[p]
beloved-in-the-East TV shows, including the popular kids'
Sandmännchen—"Little Sandman".

SOUTH OF UNTER DEN LINDEN

The following sights—heavy on Nazi and Wall history—are listed
roughly north to south (as you reach them from Unter den Linden).

▲▲Gendarmenmarkt

This delightful, historic square is bounded by twin churches, a
tasty chocolate shop, and the Berlin Symphony's concert hall (de-

signed by Karl Friedrich Schinkel, the
man who put the Neoclassical stamp
on Berlin and Dresden). In summer, it
hosts a few outdoor cafés, *Biergarten*s,
and sometimes concerts. Wonderfully
symmetrical, the square is considered
by Berliners to be the finest in town
(U6: Französische Strasse; U2 or U6:
Stadtmitte).

The name of the square, which is
part French and part German (after the *Gens d'Armes,* Frederick
the Great's royal guard, who were headquartered here), reminds us
that in the 17th century, a fifth of all Berliners were French émigrés—Protestant Huguenots fleeing Catholic France. Back then,
Frederick the Great's tolerant Prussia was a magnet for the persecuted (and their money). These émigrés vitalized Berlin with new
ideas, know-how, and their substantial wealth.

The church on the south end of square (to your left facing the
concert hall) is the **German Cathedral** (Deutscher Dom—not to
be confused with the Berlin Cathedral on Museum Island). This
cathedral was bombed flat in the war and rebuilt only in the 1980s.
It houses the thought-provoking "Milestones, Setbacks, Side-
tracks" *(Wege, Irrwege, Umwege)* exhibit, which traces the history
of the German parliamentary system—worth ▲. While light on
actual historical artifacts, the well done exhibit takes you quickly
from the revolutionary days of 1848 to the 1920s, and then more
deeply through the tumultuous 20th century. There are no English descriptions—but you can follow along with the excellent and
free 1.5-hour English audioguide (ID required). The exhibit feels
less like a museum and more like an educational exercise—because
that's just what this is. Germany is well aware that a dumbed-down
electorate, manipulated by clever spin-meisters and sound-bite
media blitzes, is a dangerous thing (free, Tue-Sun 10:00-19:00,
Oct-April until 18:00, closed Mon year-round, tel. 030/2273-
0432).

athedral (Französischer Dom), at the north ffers a humble museum on the Huguenots (€2, 0, closed Mon, enter around the right side, tel. viewpoint in the dome up top (€3, daily 10:00- until 17:30, 244 steps, enter through door facing square, tel. 030/203-060, www.franzoesischer-dom.de).

Fun fact: Neither of these churches is a true cathedral, as they never contained a bishop's throne; their German titles of *Dom* (cathedral) are actually a mistranslation from the French word *dôme* (cupola).

Fassbender & Rausch, on the corner near the German Cathedral, claims to be Europe's biggest chocolate store. After 150

years of chocolate-making, this family-owned business proudly displays its sweet delights—250 different kinds—on a 55-foot-long buffet. Truffles are sold for about €0.75 each; it's fun to compose a fancy little eight-piece box of your own. Upstairs is an elegant hot chocolate café with fine views. The window displays feature giant chocolate models of Berlin landmarks—Reichstag, Brandenburg Gate, Kaiser Wilhelm Memorial Church, a chunk of the wall, and so on. If all

this isn't enough to entice you, I have three words: erupting chocolate volcano (Mon-Sat 10:00-20:00, Sun from 11:00, corner of Mohrenstrasse at Charlottenstrasse 60, tel. 030/757-882-440).

Gendarmenmarkt is buried in what has recently emerged as Berlin's "Fifth Avenue" shopping district. For the ultimate in top-end shops, find the corner of Jägerstrasse and Friedrichstrasse and wander through the **Quartier 206** (Mon-Fri 10:30-19:30, Sat 10:00-18:00, closed Sun). The adjacent, middlebrow **Quartier 205** has more affordable prices.

Nazi and Cold War Sites near Checkpoint Charlie

A variety of fascinating sites relating to Germany's tumultuous 20th century cluster south of Unter den Linden. While you can see your choice of the following places in any order, I've linked them with walking directions from Potsdamer Platz to Checkpoint Charlie.

• *From Potsdamer Platz, take a few steps down Stresemannstrasse and*

BERLIN

detour left down Erna-Berger-Strasse to find a lonely concrete watchtower.

DDR Watchtower

This was one of many such towers built in 1966 for panoramic surveillance and shooting (note the rifle windows, allowing shots to be fired in 360 degrees). It was constantly manned by two guards who were forbidden to get to know each other (no casual chatting)—so they could effectively guard each other from escaping. This is one of only a few such towers still standing.

Cost and Hours: €3.50, open only sporadically, though officially daily 11:00-15:00.

• *Return to Stresemannstrasse, and continue south (away from Potsdamer Platz). As you round the corner turning left, you'll begin to see some...*

Fragments of the Wall

Surviving stretches of the Wall are rare in downtown Berlin, but you'll find a few in this area. On the left as you turn from Erna-Berger-Strasse onto Stresemannstrasse, look carefully at the modern Ministry of the Environment (Bundesmin-

isterium für Umwelt) building; notice the nicely painted stretch of **inner wall** (inside the modern building constructed around it). The Wall was actually two walls, with a death strip in the middle (where Stresemannstrasse is today). Across the street, embedded in the sidewalk, cobblestones mark the former path of the outer wall.

• *From here, you could continue down Stresemannstrasse and detour to the modest* **Berlin Story Bunker** *museum, located in a still-intact WWII air-raid shelter (small entry fee, closed Mon, Schöneberger Strasse 23a, www.berlinstory-bunker.de).*

But we'll continue our walk: At the corner with Niederkirchner-strasse, turn left and follow the cobbles in the sidewalk. After about a block (just beyond the Martin-Gropius-Bau museum), where the street becomes cobbled, an **original fragment** *of the Berlin Wall stretches alongside the right side of the street.*

Follow the Wall until it ends, at the intersection of Niederkirch-nerstrasse and Wilhelmstrasse. Hook right around the end of the Wall to reach the…

▲▲Topography of Terror (Topographie des Terrors)

Coincidentally, the patch of land behind the surviving stretch of Wall was closely associated with an even more deplorable re-gime: It was once the nerve center for the the Gestapo and the SS, the most despicable elements of the Nazi government. This stark, gray, boxy building is one of the few memorial sites that focuses on the perpetrators rather than the victims of the Nazis. It's chilling to see just how seam-lessly and bureaucratically the Nazi  institutions and state structures merged to become a well-oiled ter-ror machine. There are few actual artifacts here; it's mostly written explanations and photos, like reading a good textbook standing up. And, while you could read this story anywhere, to take this in atop the Gestapo headquarters is a powerful experience. The exhibit is a bit dense, but WWII historians (even armchair ones) will find it fascinating.

Cost and Hours: Free, includes audioguide for outdoor exhib-it, daily 10:00-20:00, outdoor exhibit closes at dusk, Niederkirch-nerstrasse 8, U-Bahn: Potsdamer Platz or Kochstrasse, S-Bahn: Anhalter Bahnhof or Potsdamer Platz, tel. 030/254-5090, www.topographie.de.

Background: This location marks what was once the most feared address in Berlin: the headquarters of the Reich Main Se-curity Office *(Reichssicherheitshauptamt)*. These offices served as the engine room of the Nazi dictatorship, as well as the command center of the SS (*Schutzstaffel*, whose members began as Hitler's personal bodyguards), the Gestapo (*Geheime Staatspolizei*, secret state police), and the SD (*Sicherheitsdienst*, the Nazi intelligence agency). This trio (and others) were ultimately consolidated under Heinrich Himmler to become a state-within-a-state, with talons in every corner of German society. This elite militarized branch of the Nazi machine was also tasked with the "racial purification" of German-held lands, especially Eastern Europe: the "Final Solution to the Jewish Question." It was from these headquarters that the Nazis administered concentration camps, firmed up plans for their genocide of Jews, and organized the domestic surveillance of anyone opposed to the regime. The building was also equipped with dungeons, where the Gestapo detained and tortured thousands of prisoners.

The Gestapo and SS employed intimidation techniques to coerce cooperation from the German people. The general public knew that the Gestapo was to be feared: It was considered omnipotent, omnipresent, and omniscient. Some political prisoners underwent "enhanced interrogation" right here in this building. The threat of *Schutzhaft* ("protective custody," usually at a concentration camp) was used to terrify any civilians who stepped out of line—or who might make a good example. But Hitler and his cronies also won people's loyalties through propaganda. They hammered home the idealistic notion of the *Volksgemeinschaft* ("people's community") of a purely Germanic culture and race, which empowered Hitler to create a pervasive illusion that "we're all in this together." Anyone who was not an Aryan was *Untermensch*—subhuman—and must be treated as such.

Visiting the Museum: The complex has two parts: indoors, in the modern boxy building; and outdoors, in the trench that runs along the surviving stretch of Wall. Visit the indoor exhibit first.

Inside, you'll find a visitors center with an information desk and an extensive **Topography of Terror** exhibit about the SS and Gestapo, and the atrocities they committed in Berlin and across Europe. A model of the government quarter, circa 1939, sets the stage of Nazi domination in this area. A timeline of events and old photographs, documents, and newspaper clippings illustrates how Hitler and his team expertly manipulated the German people to build a broadly supported "dictatorship of consent."

The exhibit walks you through the evolution of Hitler's regime: the Nazi takeover; institutions of terror (Himmler's "SS State"); terror, persecution, and extermination; atrocities in Nazi-occupied countries; and the war's end and postwar. Some images here are indelible, such as photos of SS soldiers stationed at Auschwitz, gleefully yukking it up on a retreat in the countryside (as their helpless prisoners were being gassed and burned a few miles

BERLIN

away). The exhibit profiles specific members of the various reprehensible SS branches, as well as the groups they targeted: Jews; Roma and Sinti (Gypsies); the unemployed or home-less; homosexuals; and the physically and mentally ill (considered "use-less eaters" who consumed resources without contributing work).

Downstairs is a WC and a library with research books on these topics. Before heading outside, ask at the information desk for the free audioguide that describes the outdoor exhibits.

Outside, in the trench along the Wall, you'll find the exhibit **Berlin 1933-1945: Between Propaganda and Terror** (occasion-

ally replaced by temporary exhibits), which overlaps slightly with the indoor ex-hibit but focuses on Berlin. The chronological survey begins with the post-WWI Weimar Republic and con-tinues through the ragged days just after World War II. One display explains how Nazis invented holidays (or injected new Aryan meaning into ex-isting ones) as a means of winning over the public. Other exhibits cover the "Aryanization" of Jewish businesses (they were simply taken over by the state and handed over to new Aryan owners); Hitler's plans for converting Berlin into a gigantic "Welthauptstadt (World Capital) Germania"; and the postwar Berlin Airlift, which brought provisions to some 2.2 million West Berliners whose sup-ply lines were cut off by East Berlin.

With more time, explore the grounds around the blocky build-ing on a **"Site Tour."** Posted signs (and the audioguide) explain 15 different locations, including the scant remains of the prison cel-lars.

• Backtrack to Niederkirchnerstrasse. Opposite the Wall remnant is one end of the huge...

German Finance Ministry (Bundesministerium der Finanzen)

The only major Hitler-era government building that survived the war's bombs, this once housed the headquarters of the Nazi Luft-waffe (Air Force). The whole building gives off a monumental feel, making the average person feel small and powerless. After the war, this was the headquarters for the Soviet occupation. Later the

DDR was founded here, and the communists used the building to house their—no joke—Ministry of Ministries.

Walk up Wilhelmstrasse (to the north) to see an entry gate (on your left) that looks much like it did when Germany occupied nearly all of Europe. This courtyard is often used by movie producers needing a Nazi set.

On the north side of the building (farther up Wilhelmstrasse, under the portico at the corner with Leipziger Strasse) is a won-

derful example of communist art. The mural, Max Lingner's *Aufbau der Republik* (*Building the Republic*, 1953), is classic Socialist Realism, showing the entire society—industrial laborers, farm workers, women, and children—all happily singing the same patriotic song. Its subtitle: "The importance of peace for the cultural development of humanity and the necessity of struggle to achieve this goal." This was the communist ideal. For the reality, look at the ground in the courtyard in front of the mural to see an enlarged photograph from a 1953 uprising here against the communists...quite a contrast. Placards explain the events of 1953 in English.

• *Retrace your steps to the Niederkirchnerstrasse intersection and hook left onto Zimmerstrasse. Continue for a block past several "Ost-algic" business ventures: vendors of DDR soft ice-cream, Trabi World (renting rides in iconic DDR tin-can cars), and the Wall Panorama Exhibition (not worth the entry fee, as it's just huge photos). You'll wind up at...*

▲Checkpoint Charlie

This famous Cold War checkpoint was not named for a person, but for its checkpoint number—as in Alpha (#1, at the East-West German border, a hundred miles west of here), Bravo (#2, as you enter Berlin proper), and Charlie (#3, the best known because most foreigners passed through here). While the actual checkpoint has long since been dismantled, its former location is home to a fine museum and a

mock-up of the original border crossing. The area has become a Cold War freak show and—as if celebrating the final victory of crass capitalism—is one of Berlin's worst tourist traps. A Mc-

Donald's stands defiantly overlooking the former haunt of East German border guards. (For a more sober and intellectually redeeming look at the Wall's history, head for the Berlin Wall Memorial at Bernauer Strasse.)

The rebuilt **guard station** now hosts two actors playing American guards who pose for photos. Notice the larger-than-life **posters** of a young American soldier facing east and a young Soviet soldier facing west. (Look carefully at the "Soviet" soldier. He was photographed in 1999, a decade after there were Soviet soldiers stationed here. He's a Dutch model. His uniform is a nonsensical pile of pins and ribbons with a Russian flag on his shoulder.)

A **photo exhibit** stretches up and down Zimmerstrasse, with great English descriptions telling the story of the Wall. While you could get this information from a book, it's certainly a different experience to stand here in person and ponder the gripping history of this place.

A few yards away (on Zimmerstrasse), a **glass panel** describes the former checkpoint. From there, another double row of **cobbles** in Zimmerstrasse shows the former path of the Wall.

Warning: Here and in other places, hustlers charge an exorbitant €10 for a full set of Cold War-era stamps in your passport. Don't be tempted. Technically, this invalidates your passport—which has caused some tourists big problems.

• *Overlooking the chaos of the street scene is the...*

▲▲Museum of the Wall at Checkpoint Charlie (Mauermuseum Haus am Checkpoint Charlie)

While the famous border checkpoint between the American and Soviet sectors is long gone, its memory is preserved by one of Europe's most cluttered museums. During the Cold War, the House at Checkpoint Charlie stood defiantly—within spitting distance of the border guards—showing off all the clever escapes over, under, and through the Wall. Today, while the drama is over and hunks of the Wall stand like trophies at its door, the museum survives as a living artifact of the Cold War days. The yellowed descriptions, which have scarcely changed since that time, tinge the museum with nostalgia. It's dusty, disorganized, and overpriced, with lots of reading involved, but all that just adds to this museum's borderline-kitschy charm. If you're pressed for time, visit after dinner, when most other museums are closed.

Cost and Hours: €12.50, assemble 20 tourists and get in for €8.50 each, €3.50 audioguide, daily 9:00-22:00, U6 to Kochstrasse

or—better from Zoo—U2 to Stadtmitte, Friedrichstrasse 43, tel. 030/253-7250, www.mauermuseum.de.

Visiting the Museum: Exhibits narrate a gripping history of the Wall, with a focus on the many ingenious **escape attempts** (the early years—with a cruder wall—saw more escapes). You'll see the actual items used to smuggle would-be Wessies: a VW bug whose trunk hid a man, two side-by-side suitcases into which a woman squeezed, a makeshift zip line for crossing over (rather than through) the border, a hot-air balloon in which two families floated to safety, an inflatable boat that puttered across the dangerous Baltic Sea, primitive homemade aircraft, two surfboards hollowed out to create just enough space for a refugee, and more. One chilling exhibit lists some 43,000 people who died in "Internal Affairs" internment camps during the transition to communism (1945-1950). Profiles personalize various escapees and their helpers, including John P. Ireland, an American who posed as an eccentric antiques collector so he could transport 10 refugees to safety in his modified Cadillac.

You'll also see **artwork** inspired by the Wall and its fall, and a memorial to Rainer Hildebrandt, who founded this museum shortly after the Wall went up in 1961. On the **top floor** (easy to miss), the exhibits broaden to the larger themes of freedom and persecution, including Eastern European rebellions (the 1956 uprising in Hungary, 1968's Prague Spring, and the Solidarity movement in 1980s Poland) and Gandhi's protests in India. Fans of the "Gipper" appreciate the room honoring President Ronald Reagan, displaying his actual cowboy hat and boots. The small movie theater shows various Wall-related films (a schedule is posted), and the displays include video coverage of those heady days when people-power tore down the Wall.

Farther South of Unter den Linden

▲▲Jewish Museum Berlin (Jüdisches Museum Berlin)

This museum is one of Europe's best Jewish sights. The highly conceptual building is a sight in itself, and the museum inside—an overview of the rich culture and history of Europe's Jewish community—is excellent, particularly if you take advantage of the informative

The Berlin Wall (and Its Fall)

The 96-mile-long "Anti-Fascist Protective Rampart"—as the Berlin Wall was called by the East German government—was erected almost overnight in 1961. It was intended to stop the outward flow of people from East to West: Three million had leaked out between 1949 and 1961. The Wall *(Mauer)* was actually two walls; the outer one, directly facing the West, was a 12-foot-high concrete barrier whose rounded, pipe-like top (to discourage grappling hooks) was adorned with plenty of barbed wire. Sandwiched between the walls was a no-man's-land "death strip" between 30 and 160 feet wide. More than 100 sentry towers kept a close eye on the Wall. On their way into the death strip, would-be escapees tripped a silent alarm, which alerted sharpshooters.

During the Wall's 28 years, border guards fired 1,693 times and made 3,221 arrests, and there were 5,043 documented successful escapes (565 of these were East German guards). At least 138 people died or were killed at the Wall while trying to escape.

As a tangible symbol for the Cold War, the Berlin Wall got a lot of attention from politicians, both East and West. Two of the 20th century's most repeated presidential quotes were uttered within earshot of the death strip. In 1963, President John F. Kennedy professed American solidarity with the struggling people of Berlin: *"Ich bin ein Berliner."* A generation later in 1987, with the stiff winds of change already blowing westward from Moscow, President Ronald Reagan issued an ultimatum to his Soviet counterpart: "Mr. Gorbachev, tear down this wall."

The actual fall of the Wall had less to do with presidential proclamations than with the obvious failings of the Soviet system, a general thawing in Moscow (where Gorbachev introduced *perestroika* and *glasnost,* and declared that he would no longer employ force to keep Eastern European satellite states under Soviet rule), the brave civil-disobedience actions of many ordinary citizens behind the Wall—and a bureaucratic snafu.

By November 1989, change was in the air. Hungary had already opened its borders to the West that summer, making it next to impossible for East German authorities to keep people in. Anti-regime protests had swept nearby Leipzig a few weeks earlier, attracting hundreds of thousands of supporters. On October 7, 1989—the 40th anniversary of the creation of the DDR—East German premier Erich Honecker said, "The Wall will be standing in 50 and even in 100 years." He was only off by 99 years and 11 months. A similar rally in East Berlin's Alexanderplatz on November 4—with a half-million protesters chanting, *"Wir wollen raus!"* (We want out!)—persuaded the East German politburo to begin a gradual process of relaxing travel restrictions.

The DDR's intention was to slightly crack the door to the West, but an inarticulate spokesman's confusion inadvertently

threw it wide open. In back-room meetings early on Thursday, November 9, officials decided they would allow a few more Easterners to cross into the West—a symbolic reform that was intended to take place gradually. The politburo members then left town early for a long weekend. The announcement of the decision was left to a spokesman, one Günter Schabowski, who knew only what was on a piece of paper handed to him moments before he went on TV for a routine press conference. At 18:54, Schabowski read the statement dutifully, with little emotion, seemingly oblivious to the massive impact of his own words: "exit via border crossings...possible for every citizen." Reporters, unable to believe what they were hearing, prodded him about when the borders would open. Schabowski looked with puzzlement at the brief statement, shrugged, and offered his best guess: *"Ab sofort, unverzüglich."* ("Immediately, without delay.")

Schabowski's words spread like wildfire through the streets of both Berlins, its flames fanned by West German TV broadcasts (and NBC's Tom Brokaw). East Berliners began to show up at Wall checkpoints, demanding that border guards let them pass. As the crowds grew, the guards could not reach anyone who could issue official orders. Finally, around 23:30, a border guard named Harald Jäger at the Bornholmer Strasse crossing decided to simply open the gates. Easterners flooded into the West, embracing their long-separated cousins, unable to believe their good fortune. Once open, the Wall could never be closed again.

The carnival atmosphere of those first years after the Wall fell is gone, but hawkers still sell "authentic" pieces of the Wall, DDR flags, and military paraphernalia to gawking tourists. When it fell, the Wall was literally carried away by the euphoria. What managed to survive has been nearly devoured by decades of persistent "Wall-peckers."

Americans—the Cold War victors—seem to have the biggest appetite for Wall-related sights, and a few bits and pieces remain for us to seek out. Berlin's best Wall-related sights are the **Berlin Wall Memorial** along Bernauer Strasse, with a long stretch of surviving Wall (see page 75), and the **Museum of the Wall at Checkpoint Charlie** (see page 64). Other stretches of the Wall still standing include the short section at Niederkirchnerstrasse/Wilhelmstrasse (near the Topography of Terror exhibit; page 60), in the Mauerpark in Prenzlauer Berg, and the longer East Side Gallery (near the Ostbahnhof; page 80).

and engaging audioguide. Rather than just reading dry texts, you'll feel this museum as fresh and alive—an exuberant celebration of the Jewish experience that's accessible to all. Even though the museum is in a nondescript residential neighborhood, it's well worth the trip.

Cost and Hours: €8, daily 10:00-20:00, Mon until 22:00, last entry one hour before closing, closed on Jewish holidays. Tight security includes bag check and metal detectors. The excellent €3 audioguide—with four hours of commentary—is essential to fully appreciate the exhibits. Tel. 030/2599-3300, www.jmberlin.de.

Getting There: Take the U-Bahn to Hallesches Tor, find the exit marked *Jüdisches Museum,* exit straight ahead, then turn right on Franz-Klühs-Strasse. The museum is a five-minute walk ahead on your left, at Lindenstrasse 9.

Eating: The museum's restaurant, Café Schmus, offers good Jewish-style meals, albeit not kosher (daily 10:00-20:00, Mon until 22:00).

Visiting the Museum: Designed by American architect Daniel Libeskind (the master planner for the redeveloped World Trade Center in New York), the zinc-walled building has a zigzag shape pierced by voids symbolic of the irreplaceable cultural loss caused by the Holocaust. Enter the 18th-century Baroque building next door, then go through an underground tunnel to reach the museum interior.

Before you reach the exhibit, your visit starts with three **memorial spaces.** Follow the Axis of Exile to a disorienting slanted garden with 49 pillars (evocative of the Memorial to the Murdered Jews of Europe, across town). Next, the Axis of Holocaust, lined with artifacts from Jews imprisoned and murdered by the Nazis, leads to an eerily empty tower shut off from the outside world. The Axis of Continuity takes you to stairs and the main exhibit. A detour partway up the long stairway leads to the Memory Void, a compelling space of "fallen leaves": heavy metal faces that you walk on, making unhuman noises with each step.

Finish climbing the stairs to the top of the museum, and stroll chronologically through the 2,000-year **story of Judaism** in Germany. The exhibit, on two floors, is engaging, with lots of actual artifacts. Interactive bits (you can, for example, spell your name in Hebrew, or write a prayer and hang it from a tree) make it lively for kids. English explanations interpret both the exhibits and the design of the very symbolic building.

The top floor focuses on everyday life in Ashkenaz (medieval

German-Jewish lands). The nine-minute movie *A Thousand Years Ago* sets the stage for your journey through Jewish history. You'll learn what garlic had to do with early Jews in Germany (hint: It's not just about cooking). The Middle Ages were a positive time for Jewish culture, which flourished then in many areas of Europe. But around 1500, many Jews were expelled from the countryside and moved into cities. Viewing stations let you watch nine short, lively videos that pose provocative questions about faith. Moses Mendelssohn's role in the late-18th-century Jewish Enlightenment, which gave rise to Reform Judaism, is highlighted. The Tradition and Change exhibit analyzes how various subgroups of the Jewish faith modified and relaxed their rules to adapt to a changing world.

Downstairs, on the middle floor, exhibits detail the rising tide of anti-Semitism in Germany through the 19th century—at a time when many Jews were so secularized that they celebrated Christmas right along with Hanukkah. Berlin's glory days (1890-1933) were a boom time for many Jews, though it was at times challenging to reconcile the reformed ways of the more assimilated western (German) Jews with the more traditional Eastern European Jews. The exhibit segues into the **dark days** of Hitler—the collapse of the relatively tolerant Weimar Republic, the rise of the Nazis, and the horrific night of November 9, 1938, when, throughout Germany, hateful mobs destroyed Jewish-owned businesses, homes, synagogues, and even entire villages—called "Crystal Night" (Kristallnacht) for the broken glass that glittered in the streets.

The display brings us to the present day, with the question: How do you keep going after six million of your people have been murdered? You'll see how German society reacted to the two largest Nazi trials, complete with historical film clips of the perpetrators. In the last segment, devoted to Jewish life today, German Jews describe their experiences growing up in the postwar years.

Kreuzberg

This district—once abutting the dreary Wall and inhabited mostly by poor Turkish guest laborers and their families—is still rundown, with graffiti-riddled buildings and plenty of student and Turkish street life. It offers a gritty look at melting-pot Berlin, in a city where original Berliners are as rare as old buildings. Berlin is the largest Turkish city outside of Turkey itself, and Kreuzberg is its "downtown." But to call it a "little Istanbul" insults the big one. You'll see *Döner Kebab* stands, shops decorated with spray paint, and mothers wrapped in colorful scarves. Lately, an influx of immigrants from many other countries has diluted the Turkish-ness of Kreuzberg. For the most colorful experience, visit on Tuesday or Friday between 11:00 and 18:30, when the **Turkish Market** sprawls along Maybachufer street beside the Landwehr Canal.

Take the U-Bahn to Kottbusser Tor and wander down Kottbusser Strasse, cross the canal, and turn left down Maybachufer.

HACKESCHER MARKT AND ORANIENBURGER STRASSE

This area is light on major sights but has some of Berlin's trendiest, most interesting neighborhoods. I've listed these roughly from south to north, as you'd approach them from the city center. On a sunny day, a stroll (or tram ride) through these bursting-with-life areas can be as engaging as any museum in town.

Hackescher Markt

This area, in front of the S-Bahn station of the same name, is a great people scene day and night. The brick trestle supporting the train track is a classic example of the city's Brandenburg Neo-Gothic brickwork. Most of the brick archways are now filled with hip shops, which have official—and trendy—addresses such as "S-Bahn Arch #9, Hackescher Markt." Within 100 yards of the S-Bahn station, you'll find recommended Turkish and Bavarian restaurants, walking-tour and pub-crawl departure points, and tram #M1 to Prenzlauer Berg. Also nearby are two fascinating examples of Berlin's traditional courtyards *(Höfe)*—one trendy and modern, the other retro-cool, with two fascinating museums.

Hackesche Höfe

A block in front of the Hackescher Markt S-Bahn station (at Rosenthaler Strasse 40) is a series of eight courtyards bunny-hopping through a wonderfully restored 1907 *Jugendstil* (German Art Nouveau) building. Berlin's apartments are organized like this—courtyard after courtyard leading off the main road. This complex is full of artsy designer shops, popular restaurants (including the recommended Turkish eatery, Hasir), theaters, and cinemas. Courtyard #5 is particularly charming, with a children's park, and an Ampelmann store. This courtyard system is a wonderful example of how to make huge city blocks livable. Two decades after the Cold War, this area has reached the final evolution of East Berlin's urban restoration: total gentrification. These courtyards also offer a useful lesson for visitors: Much of Berlin's charm hides off the street front.

Haus Schwarzenberg

Next door (at Rosenthaler Strasse 39), this courtyard has a totally different feel. Owned by an artists' collective, it comes with a bar, cinema, open-air art space (reminiscent of mid-1990s eastern Berlin), and the basement-level "Dead Chickens" gallery (with far-out hydro-powered art). Its Café Cinema is one of the last remaining '90s bohemian-chic bars. And within this amazing little zone you'll

Stolpersteine (Stumbling Stones)

As you wander through the Hackesche Höfe and Oranienburger Strasse neighborhoods—and throughout Europe—you

might stumble over small brass plaques in the sidewalk called *Stolpersteine*. *Stolpern* means "to stumble," which is what you are meant to do. These plaques mark the former homes of Jewish and other WWII victims of the Nazis. The *Stolpersteine* are meant not only to honor and personalize the victims, but also to stimulate thought and discussion. In addition, they're a meaningful rebuke to a prewar slur: When non-Jews tripped on a protruding rock or cobble, it was the custom among some Germans to say, "A Jew must be buried here." The *Stolpersteine* turn this idiom around, creating individual monuments to those who have no graves to mark their unjust deaths.

More than 50,000 of these plaques have been installed across Europe, mostly in Germany. They're made of brass so they stay polished as you walk over them. On each plaque is the name of the victim who lived in that spot, and how and where that person died. While some Holocaust memorials formerly used neutral terminology like "perished," now they use words like "murdered" *(ermordet)*—part of the very honest way in which today's Germans are dealing with their country's past. Installation of a *Stolperstein* can be sponsored for €120 and has become popular in schools, where students research the memorialized person's life as a class project.

find two inspirational museums. The **Museum of Otto Weidt's Workshop for the Blind** (Museum Blindenwerkstatt Otto Weidt) vividly tells the amazing story of a Berliner heroically protecting blind and deaf Jews during World War II (free, daily 10:00-20:00). Otto Weidt employed them to produce brooms and brushes, and because that was useful for the Nazi war machine, he managed to finagle a special status for his workers. You can see the actual brushmaking factory with pedal-powered machines still lined up. The exhibits are described well (in English and Braille), and there's a good intro video and free audioguide. The **Silent Heroes Memorial Center** (Gedenkstätte Stille Helden) is a well-presented exhibit celebrating the quietly courageous individuals who resisted the persecution of the Jews from 1933 to 1945 (free, daily 10:00-20:00). (A third museum here, the **Anne Frank Center,** is primarily geared toward kids...and offers almost no history on Berlin itself.)

Oranienburger Strasse

Oranienburger Strasse, a few blocks west of Hackescher Markt, is anchored by an important and somber sight, the New Synagogue. But the rest of this zone (roughly between the synagogue and Torstrasse) is colorful and quirky—especially after dark. The streets behind Grosse Hamburger Strasse flicker with atmospheric cafés, *Kneipen* (pubs), and art galleries. At night (from about 20:00), techno-prostitutes line Oranienburger Strasse. Prostitution is legal throughout Germany. Prostitutes pay taxes and receive health care insurance like anyone else. On this street, they hire security guards (lingering nearby) for safety. The sex workers all seem to buy their Barbarella wardrobes—notice the uniforms complete with matching fanny packs—at the same place.

▲New Synagogue (Neue Synagogue)

A shiny gilded dome marks the New Synagogue, now a museum and cultural center. Consecrated in 1866, this was once the biggest and finest synagogue in Germany, with seating for 3,200 worshippers and a sumptuous Moorish-style interior modeled after the Alhambra in Granada, Spain. It was desecrated by Nazis on Crystal Night (Kristallnacht) in 1938, bombed in 1943, and partially rebuilt in 1990. Only the dome and facade have been  restored—a window overlooks the vacant field marking what used to be the synagogue. On its facade, a small plaque—added by East Berlin Jews in 1966—reads "Never forget" *(Vergesst es nie)*. At that time East Berlin had only a few hundred Jews, but now that the city is reunited, the Jewish community numbers about 12,000.

Inside, past tight security, the small but moving permanent exhibit called Open Ye the Gates describes the Berlin Jewish community through the centuries (filling three big rooms on the ground floor and first floor, with some good English descriptions). Examine the cutaway model showing the entire synagogue and an exhibit of religious items. Stairs lead up (past temporary exhibits, with a separate entry fee) to the dome, where there's not much to see except the unimpressive-from-the-inside dome itself and ho-hum views—not worth the entry price or the climb.

Cost and Hours: Main exhibit-€5, dome-€3, combo-ticket for both-€6, temporary exhibits-€3, April-Oct Mon-Fri 10:00-18:00, Sun until 19:00; Oct-March exhibit only Sun-Thu 10:00-18:00, Fri until 15:00; closed Sat year-round; audioguide-€3, Oranienburger Strasse 28/30, enter through the low-profile door in the modern building just right of the domed synagogue facade,

S-Bahn: Oranienburger Strasse, tel. 030/8802-8300 and press 1, www.cjudaicum.de.

Eating: Next door to the New Synagogue (to the left as you face it) is every local kid's favorite traditional candy shop, **Bonbonmacherei,** where you can see candy being made the old-fashioned way (Wed-Sat 12:00-19:00, closed Sun-Tue and often July-Aug, at Oranienburger Strasse 32, in the Heckmann Höfe—another classic Berlin courtyard). And just around the corner and down the street from the synagogue, you'll find the fully kosher **Beth Café** (closed Sat, Tucholskystrasse 40).

Nearby: A block from the synagogue (to the right as you face it), walk 50 yards down **Grosse Hamburger Strasse** to a little park. This street was known for 200 years as the "street of tolerance" because the Jewish community donated land to Protestants so they could build a church. Hitler turned it into the "street of death" *(Todesstrasse),* bulldozing 12,000 graves of the city's oldest Jewish cemetery and turning a Jewish nursing home into a deportation center. Because of the small but growing radical Islamic element in Berlin, and a smattering of persistent neo-Nazis, several police officers and an Israeli secret agent keep watch over the Jewish high school nearby.

The Kennedys Museum

This crisp, private enterprise (in a former Jewish girls' school building that survived the war) delightfully recalls John F. Kennedy's 1963 Germany trip with great photos and video clips as well as a photographic shrine to the Kennedy clan in America. Among the interesting mementos are old campaign buttons and posters, and JFK's notes with the phonetic pronunciation "Ish bin ein Bearleener." Jacqueline Kennedy commented on how strange it was that this—not even in his native language—was her husband's most quotable quote. The highlight: a theater where you can watch a newsreel of Kennedy's historic speech (20 minutes, plays continuously).

Cost and Hours: €5, Tue-Sun 11:00-19:00, closed Mon, tel. 030/2065-3570, www.thekennedys.de. From Oranienburger Strasse, go a block up Tucholskystrasse and turn right to find the dark-brick building three doors down at Auguststrasse 13 (doors may be closed but walk right in through entryway, then head to the right and up two floors).

▲▲PRENZLAUER BERG AND NEARBY

Young, in-the-know locals agree that Prenzlauer Berg is one of Berlin's most colorful neighborhoods. The heart of this area, with a dense array of hip cafés, restaurants, boutiques, and street life, is roughly between Helmholtzplatz and Kollwitzplatz and along

Kastanienallee (U2: Senefelderplatz and Eberswalder Strasse; or take the S-Bahn to Hackescher Markt and catch tram #M1 north).

"Prenzl'berg," as Berliners call it, was largely untouched during World War II, but its buildings slowly rotted away under the communists. Then, after the Wall fell, it was overrun first with artists and anarchists, then with laid-back hipsters, energetic young families, and clever entrepreneurs who breathed life back into its classic old apartment blocks, deserted factories, and long-forgotten breweries.

Years of rent control kept things affordable for its bohemian residents. But now landlords are free to charge what the market will bear, and the vibe is changing. This is ground zero for Berlin's baby boom: Tattooed and pierced young moms and dads, who've joined the modern rat race without giving up their alternative flair, push their youngsters in designer strollers past trendy boutiques and restaurants.

Aside from the **Berlin Wall Memorial** at its western edge (see below), the neighborhood has few real sights—just a lively, laid-back neighborhood ignoring its wonderful late-19th-century architecture high overhead. The intersection of Oderberger Strasse and Kastanienallee is a typically convivial bit of Prenzlauer Berg to explore.

If you walk west to the end of Oderberger Strasse, you'll hit the **Mauerpark** (Wall Park). Once part of the Wall's death strip,

today it's a Prenzlauer Berg green space—an alternative promenade. The park is particularly entertaining on Sundays, when it hosts a rummage market and a giant karaoke party. Along the bluff runs a bit of the Wall covered in graffiti art. Just beyond that is the Friedrich-Ludwig-Jahn-Sportpark stadium from DDR times, built to host the World Youth Festival in 1951 and still marked by its original bombastic light towers (even light towers were designed to stir young communist souls). To the southwest are the outdoor exhibits of the Berlin Wall Memorial.

Berliners have a strong sense of community. They manage this in a big city by enjoying a strong neighborhood identity in areas like Prenzlauer Berg. But there is some tension these days, as locals complain about cafés and bars catering to yuppies sipping prosecco, while working-class and artistic types are being priced out.

While it has changed plenty, I find Prenzlauer Berg a celebra-

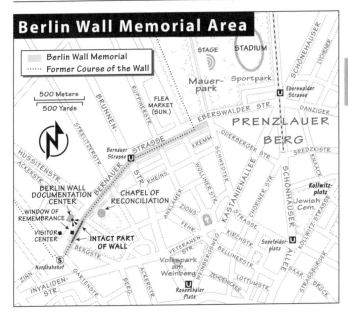

Berlin Wall Memorial Area

- Berlin Wall Memorial
- ····· Former Course of the Wall

tion of life and a joy to stroll through. It's a fun area to explore, people-watch, shop, have a meal or spend the night.

▲▲▲Berlin Wall Memorial (Gedenkstätte Berliner Mauer)

While tourists flock to Checkpoint Charlie, this memorial is Berlin's most substantial attraction relating to its gone-but-not-forgotten Wall. Exhibits line up along several blocks of Bernauer Strasse, stretching northeast from the Nordbahnhof S-Bahn station. You can enter two different museums plus various open-air exhibits and memorials, see several fragments of the Wall, and peer from an observation tower down into a preserved, complete stretch of the Wall system (as it was during the Cold War).

The Berlin Wall, which was erected virtually overnight in 1961, ran right along Bernauer Strasse. People were suddenly separated from their neighbors across the street. This stretch was particularly notorious because existing apartment buildings were incorporated into the structure of the Wall itself. Film footage and photographs from the era show Berliners worriedly watching workmen seal off these buildings from the West, brick by brick. Some people attempted to leap to freedom from upper-story windows, with mixed results. One of the unfortunate ones was Ida Siekmann, who fell to her death from her third-floor apartment on August 22, 1961, and is considered the first casualty of the Berlin Wall.

Cost and Hours: Free; Visitor Center and Documentation Center open Tue-Sun 10:00-18:00, closed Mon, outdoor areas accessible 24 hours daily, memorial chapel closes at 17:00; Bernauer Strasse 111, tel. 030/4679-86666, www.berliner-mauer-gedenkstaette.de.

Getting There: Take the S-Bahn (line S-1, S-2, or S-25—all handy from Potsdamer Platz, Brandenburger Tor, Friedrichstrasse, Oranienburger Strasse, or Hackescher Markt) to the Nordbahnhof. The Nordbahnhof's underground hallways have history exhibits in English (explained later). Exit by following signs for *Bernauer Strasse*. You'll pop out across the street from a long chunk of Wall and kitty-corner from the Visitor Center.

Visiting the Memorial: From the Nordbahnhof station (which has some interesting Wall history in itself), head first to the Visitor Center to get your bearings, then explore the assorted Wall fragments and other sights in the park across the street. Work your way up Bernauer Strasse to the Documentation Center, Wall System, memorial chapel, and remaining signposts (look for the escape-tunnel paths marked in the grass),  until you reach the Bernauer Strasse U-Bahn station (or continue beyond the U-Bahn stop to see all the outdoor exhibits, which stretch up to the Mauerpark).

Nordbahnhof: This S-Bahn station was one of the "ghost stations" of Cold War Berlin. It was built in 1926, closed in 1961, and opened again in 1989. As it was a dogleg of the East mostly surrounded by the West, Western subway trains had permission to use the underground tracks to zip through this station (without stopping, of course) en route between stops in the West. Posted information boards show photos comparing 1989 with 2009, and explain that East German border guards, who were stationed here to ensure that nobody got on or off those trains, were locked into their surveillance rooms to prevent them from escaping. (But one subway employee and his family used the tunnels to walk to the West and freedom.)

Follow signs down a long yellow hall to Bernauer Strasse. Climbing the stairs up to the Bernauer Strasse exit, ponder that the doorway at the top of these stairs (marked by the *Sperrmauer 1961-1989* plaque) was a bricked-off no-man's-land just 26 years ago. Stepping outside, you'll see a park full of outdoor exhibits (directly across the street) and the Visitor Center (in a low rust-colored building kitty-corner across the street).

Visitor Center (Bezucherzentrum): This small complex has a helpful information desk, and two good movies that provide context for a visit (they run in English at :30 after the hour, about 30 minutes for the whole spiel): *The Berlin Wall* offers a great 15-minute overview of its history. That's followed by *Walled In!,* an animated 12-minute film illustrating the Wall as it functioned here at Bernauer Strasse. Before leaving, pick up the brochures explaining the outdoor exhibits.

Wall Fragments and Other Sights: Across the street from the Visitor Center is a long stretch of Wall. The park behind it is scattered with a few more Wall chunks as well as monuments and memorials honoring its victims, with clumps of info-posts offering brief personal stories and bits of background information (most of it available in English). To get your bearings, find the small model of the entire area when the Wall still stood (just across the street from the Nordbahnhof). While most items are accompanied by English explanations, the brochure from the Visitor Center helps you better appreciate what you're seeing. The rusty "Window of Remembrance" monument honors slain would-be escapees with their names, dates of death, and transparent photos that are viewable from both sides. Before it was the no-man's-land between the walls, this area was the parish graveyard for a nearby church; ironically, DDR officials had to move a thousand graves from here to create a "death strip."

Berlin Wall Documentation Center (Dokumentationszentrum Berliner Mauer): The center's excellent **exhibit,** recently overhauled on the 25th anniversary of the Wall's fall, is geared to a new generation of Berliners who can hardly imagine their hometown split so brutally in two. The ground floor details the logistics of the city's division and its effects on Berliners. Have a seat and listen to the riveting personal accounts of escapees—and of the border guards armed with machine guns and tasked with stopping them. The next floor up gives the historical and political context behind the Wall's construction and eventual destruction. Photos let you track the progression of changes at this exact site from 1965 to 1990.

Leaving the exhibit, climb the open-air staircase to an observation deck that gives you a bird's-eye view of the last remaining stretch of the complete wall system—guard tower, barbed wire, and all.

Stretch of Intact Wall System: This is the last surviving intact bit of the complete "Wall system" (with both sides of its Wall—capped by the round pipe that made it tougher for escapees to get a grip—and its no-man's-land death strip). The guard tower

came from a different part of the Wall; it was actually purchased on that great capitalist invention, eBay (somewhere, Stalin spins in his grave). View it from the observation deck, then visit it from ground level, where wall panels explain each part of the system. Plaques along the sidewalk mark the locations of escapes or deaths.

Chapel of Reconciliation (Kapelle der Versöhnung): Just beyond the Wall section (to the left), this chapel marks the spot of the late-19th-century Church of Reconciliation, which survived WWII bombs—but not the communists. Notice the larger footprint of the original church in the field around the chapel. When the Wall was built, the church wound up right in the middle of the death strip. It was torn down in 1985, supposedly  because it got in the way of the border guards' sight lines. (This coincided with a period in which anti-DDR opposition movements were percolating in Christian churches, prompting the atheistic regime to destroy several houses of worship.) Inside the church, the carved wooden altarpiece was saved from the original structure. The chapel hosts daily prayer services for the victims of the Wall.

Outdoor Exhibits: The memorial also includes a string of open-air exhibits along Bernauer Strasse that stretch all the way from the Nordbahnhof to the intersection with Schwedter Strasse and Oderberger Strasse, near the Mauerpark, at the heart of Prenzlauer Berg. Video and audio clips, photos, and huge photographic murals let you in on more stories of the Wall—many of which took place right where you're standing.

TO THE EAST, BEYOND ALEXANDERPLATZ
Karl-Marx-Allee

The buildings along Karl-Marx-Allee in East Berlin (just beyond Alexanderplatz) were completely leveled by the Red Army in 1945. As an expression of their adoration to the "great Socialist Father" (Stalin), the DDR government decided to rebuild the street better than ever (the USSR provided generous subsidies). They intentionally made it one meter wider than the Champs-Elysées, named it Stalinallee, and lined it with "workers' palaces" built in the bold "Stalin Gothic" style so common in Moscow in the 1950s. Now renamed after Karl Marx, the street and its restored buildings provide a rare look at Berlin's communist days. Distances are a bit long for convenient walking, but you can cruise Karl-Marx-Allee by taxi, or ride the U-Bahn to Strausberger Platz (which was built to resemble an Italian promenade) and walk to Frankfurter Tor, reading the good information posts along the way. Notice the Social Realist reliefs on the buildings and the lampposts, which incorporate the wings of a phoenix (rising from the ashes) in their design. Once a "workers' paradise," the street now hosts a two-mile-long capitalist beer festival the first weekend in August.

The **Café Sibylle,** just beyond the Strausberger Platz U-Bahn station, is a fun spot for a coffee, traditional DDR ice-cream treats, and a look at its free informal museum that tells the story of the most destroyed street in Berlin. While the humble exhibit is nearly all in German, it's fun to see the ear (or buy a plaster replica) and half a moustache from what was the largest statue of Stalin in Germany (the centerpiece of the street until 1961). It also provides a few intimate insights into apartment life in a DDR flat. The café is known for its good coffee and *Schwedeneisbecher mit Eierlikor*—an ice-cream sundae with a shot of egg liqueur, popular among those nostalgic for communism (daily 10:00-20:00, Karl-Marx-Allee 72, at intersection with Koppenstrasse, a block from U-Bahn: Strausberger Platz, tel. 030/2935-2203).

Heading out to Karl-Marx-Allee (just beyond the TV Tower), you're likely to notice a giant colorful **mural** decorating a blocky communist-era skyscraper. This was the Ministry of Education, and the mural is a tile mosaic trumpeting the accomplishments of the DDR's version of "No Child Left Behind."

Stasi Museum

This modest exhibit tells the story of how the communist-era Ministry for State Security (*Staatssicherheit,* a.k.a. Stasi)—headquartered in these very buildings—infiltrated all aspects of German life. Soon after the Wall fell, DDR authorities scrambled to destroy the copious illicit information their agents and informants had collected about the people of East Germany. But the government mandated that these records be preserved as evidence of DDR crimes, and the documents are now managed by the Federal Commissioner for Stasi Records.

Cost and Hours: €6, Mon-Fri 10:00-18:00, Sat-Sun 11:00-18:00, Ruscherstrasse 103, U5: Magdalenenstrasse, tel. 030/553-6854, www.stasimuseum.de.

Other Stasi Sights: If you're particularly keen you can trek a bit north to the Stasi Prison, where "enemies of the state" served time (€5, visits possible only with tour; English tours daily at 14:30,

April-Oct also at 11:30—call to confirm before making the trip; German tours usually hourly; Genslerstrasse 66, reachable via tram from downtown—see website for specifics, tel. 030/9860-8230, www.stiftung-hsh.de). There's also a good Stasi Museum in the former State Security branch in Leipzig, an easy day trip from Berlin.

East Side Gallery

The biggest remaining stretch of the Wall is now the "world's longest outdoor art gallery." It stretches for nearly a mile and is covered with murals painted by artists from around the world. The murals (classified as protected monuments) got a facelift in 2009, when the city invited the original artists back to re-create their work for the 20th anniversary of the fall of the Wall. This segment of the Wall makes a poignant walk. For a quick look, take the S-Bahn to the Ostbahnhof station (follow signs to Stralauerplatz exit; once outside, TV Tower will be to your right; go left and at next corner look to your right—the Wall is across the busy street). The gallery, located on the southern end of the quickly gentrifying Friedrichshain neighborhood, is slowly being consumed by developers. If you walk the entire length of the East Side Gallery, you'll find a small Wall souvenir shop at the end and a bridge crossing the river to a subway station at Schlesisches Tor (in Kreuzberg). The bridge, a fine example of Brandenburg Neo-Gothic brickwork, has a fun neon "rock, paper, scissors" installment poking fun at the futility of the Cold War (visible only after dark). For the history of the East Side Gallery, see www.eastsidegallery.com.

Sights in Central Berlin

TIERGARTEN PARK AND NEARBY

Berlin's "Central Park" stretches two miles from Bahnhof Zoo to the Brandenburg Gate.

Victory Column (Siegessäule)

The Tiergarten's centerpiece, the Victory Column, was built to commemorate the Prussian defeat of Denmark in 1864...then reinterpreted after the defeat of France in 1870. The pointy-helmeted Germans rubbed it in, decorating the tower with French cannons and paying for it all with francs received as war reparations. The three lower rings commemorate Bismarck's victories. I imagine the statues of German military greats—which lurk among the trees nearby—goose-stepping around the floodlit angel at night.

Originally standing at the Reichstag, in 1938 the tower was moved to this position and given a 25-foot lengthening by Hitler's architect, Albert Speer, in anticipation of the planned

re-envisioning of Berlin as "Welthauptstadt Germania"—the capital of a worldwide Nazi empire. Streets leading to the circle are flanked by surviving Nazi guardhouses, built in the stern style that fascists loved. At the memorial's first level, notice how WWII bullets chipped the fine marble columns. From 1989 to 2003, the column was the epicenter of the Love Parade (Berlin's city-wide techno-hedonist street party), and it was the backdrop for Barack Obama's summer 2008 visit to Germany as a presidential candidate.

Climbing its 270 steps earns you a breathtaking Berlin-wide view and a close-up of the gilded bronze statue of the goddess Victoria. You might recognize Victoria from Wim Wenders' 1987 art-house classic *Wings of Desire*, or the *Stay (Faraway, So Close!)* video he directed for the rock band U2.

Cost and Hours: Free to view from outside, €3 to climb, daily April-Oct 9:30-18:30, until 19:00 Sat-Sun, Nov-March 10:00-17:00, closes in the rain, no elevator, bus #100, tel. 030/391-2961.

German Resistance Memorial (Gedenkstätte Deutscher Widerstand)

This memorial and museum, located in the former Bendlerblock military headquarters just south of the Tiergarten, tells the story of several organized German resistance movements and the more than 42 separate assassination attempts against Hitler. While the exhibit has no real artifacts, the building itself is important: One of the most thoroughly planned schemes to kill Hitler was plotted here (the actual attempt occurred in Rastenburg, eastern Prussia). That attempt failed and several leaders of the conspiracy, including Claus Schenk Graf von Stauffenberg, were shot here in the courtyard.

Cost and Hours: Free, Mon-Fri 9:00-18:00, Thu until 20:00, Sat-Sun 10:00-18:00, free and good English audioguide, €4 printed English translation, no crowds; near Kulturforum at Stauffenberg-strasse 13, enter in courtyard, door on left, main exhibit on second floor up; bus #M29, tel. 030/2699-5000, www.gdw-berlin.de.

POTSDAMER PLATZ AND NEARBY

The "Times Square of Berlin," and possibly the busiest square in Europe before World War II, Potsdamer Platz was cut in two by the Wall and left a deserted no-man's-land for 40 years. Today, this immense commercial/residential/entertainment center, sitting on a futuristic transportation hub, is home to the European headquarters of several big-league companies.

▲Potsdamer Platz

The new Potsdamer Platz was a vision begun in 1991, the year that Germany's parliament voted to relocate the seat of government to Berlin. Since then, Sony, Daimler, and other major corporations have turned the square once again into a city center. Like great Christian churches built upon pagan holy grounds, Potsdamer Platz—with its corporate logos flying high and shiny above what was the Wall—trumpets the triumph of capitalism.

Though Potsdamer Platz had been envisioned as a new common center for Berlin, the city has always been—and remains—a scattered collection of towns. Locals recognize 28 distinct neighborhoods that may have grown together but still maintain their historic orientation. While Munich has the single dominant Marienplatz, Berlin will always have Charlottenburg, Savignyplatz, Kreuzberg, Prenzlauer Berg, and so on. In general, Berliners prefer these characteristic neighborhoods to an official city center. They're unimpressed by the grandeur of Potsdamer Platz, simply considering it a good place to go to the movies, with overpriced, touristy restaurants.

While most of the buildings here just feel big (the nearby shopping arcade is like any huge, modern, American mall), the Sony Center is worth at least a peek, and German-film buffs will enjoy the Deutsche Kinemathek museum (described later).

For an overview of the square and a scenic route to the Sony Center, start at the Bahnhof Potsdamer Platz (east end of Potsdamer Strasse, S-Bahn and U-Bahn: Potsdamer Platz, exit following *Leipziger Platz* signs to see the best view of skyscrapers as you emerge). Find the green hexagonal **clock tower** with the traffic lights on top. This is a replica of the first electronic traffic light in Europe, which once stood at the six-street intersection of Potsdamer Platz. (The traffic cops who stood with flag and trumpet in the middle of the intersection were getting hit by cars too routinely, so this perch was built for them.)

On either side of Potsdamer Strasse, you'll see enormous cubical entrances to the underground Potsdamer Platz train station. Near these entrances, notice the slanted **glass cylinders** sticking out of the ground. Mirrors on the tops of the tubes move with the sun to collect light and send it underground (saving piles of euros in energy costs). Two subtle lines in the pavement indicate where the **Berlin Wall** once stood (they trace about 25 miles of the wall through the city). On the right side of the street, notice the re-erected slabs of the Wall. Imagine when the first piece was cut out (see photo and history on nearby panel). These hang like scalps at the gate of Fort Capitalism. Look up at the towering corporate headquarters: Market forces have won a clear victory. Now descend into one of the train station entrances and follow *DB Zentrum*, then *Sony Center* signs. As you walk through the passage, notice the wall panels with historical information.

You'll come up the escalator into the **Sony Center** under a grand canopy (designed to evoke Mount Fuji). At night, multi-

colored floodlights play on the underside of this tent. Office workers and tourists eat here by the fountain, enjoying the parade of people. The modern Bavarian Lindenbräu beer hall—the Sony boss wanted a *Brauhaus*—serves traditional food. Across the plaza, Josty Bar is built around a surviving bit of a venerable hotel that was a meeting place for Berlin's rich and famous before the bombs. CineStar is a rare cinema that plays mainstream movies in their original language (www.cinestar.de).

A huge **screen** above the Deutsche Kinemathek museum (left of Starbucks) shows big sporting events on special occasions. Otherwise it runs historic video clips of Potsdamer Platz through the decades.

▲Deutsche Kinemathek Film and TV Museum

This exhibit is the most interesting place to visit in the Sony Center. The early pioneers in filmmaking were German (including Fritz Lang, F. W. Murnau, Ernst Lubitsch, and the Austrian-born Billy Wilder), and many of them also became influential in Hollywood—making this a fun visit for cinephiles. Your admission ticket gets you into several floors of exhibits (including temporary exhibits on floors 1 and 4) made meaningful by the essential English audioguide.

Cost and Hours: €7, free Thu 16:00-20:00, Tue-Sun 10:00-18:00, Thu until 20:00, closed Mon, audioguide-€2, tel. 030/300-9030, www.deutsche-kinemathek.de.

Visiting the Museum: From the ticket desk, ride the elevator up to the third floor, where you can turn left (into the film section, floors 3 and 2) or right (into the TV section, floors 3 and 4).

In the **film section,** you'll walk back in time, starting with the German film industry's beginnings, with an emphasis on the Weimar Republic period in the 1920s, when Berlin rivaled Hollywood. Influential films included the early German Expressionist masterpiece *The Cabinet of Dr. Caligari* (1920) and Fritz Lang's seminal *Metropolis* (1927). Three rooms are dedicated to Marlene Dietrich, who was a huge star both in Germany and, later, in Hollywood. (Dietrich, who performed at USO shows to entertain Allied troops fighting against her former homeland, once said, "I don't hate the Germans, I hate the Nazis.") Another section examines Nazi use of film as propaganda, including Leni Riefenstahl's masterful documentary of the 1936 Berlin Olympics and her earlier, chillingly propagandistic *Triumph des Willens (Triumph of the Will,* 1935). The postwar period was defined by two separate East and West German film industries. The exhibit's finale reminds us that German filmmakers are still highly influential and successful—including Wolfgang Petersen *(Das Boot, Air Force One, The Perfect Storm)* and Werner Herzog (documentaries such as *Grizzly Man,* and the drama *Rescue Dawn).* If a visit here gets you curious about German cinema, see the recommendations in the Appendix.

The **TV section** tells the story of *das Idioten Box* from its infancy (when it was primarily used as a Nazi propaganda tool) to today. The 30-minute kaleidoscopic review—kind of a frantic fast-forward montage of greatest hits in German TV history, both East and West—is great fun even if you don't understand a word of it (it plays all day long, with 10-minute breaks). Otherwise, the TV section is a little more challenging for non-German speakers to appreciate. Upstairs (on the fourth floor) is a TV archive where you can dial through a wide range of new and classic German TV standards.

Nearby: The Kino Arsenal theater downstairs shows offbeat art-house films in their original language.

Panoramapunkt

Across Potsdamer Strasse from the Deutsche Kinemathek museum, you can ride what's billed as the "fastest elevator in Europe" to skyscraping rooftop views. You'll travel at nearly 30 feet per second to the top of the 300-foot-tall Kollhoff Tower. Its sheltered but open-air view deck provides a fun opportunity to survey Berlin's ongoing construction from above.

Cost and Hours: €6.50, €10.50 VIP ticket lets you skip the line, daily 10:00-20:00, until 18:00 in winter, last elevator 30 minutes before closing, in red-brick building at Potsdamer Platz 1, tel. 030/2593-7080, www.panoramapunkt. de.

KULTURFORUM COMPLEX

Just west of Potsdamer Platz, Kulturforum rivals Museum Island as the city's cultural heart, with several top museums and Berlin's concert hall—home of the world-famous Berlin Philharmonic orchestra. Of its sprawling museums, only the Gemäldegalerie is a must. Its New National Gallery is closed through at least 2017.

Combo-Tickets: All Kulturforum sights are covered by a single €12 Bereichskarte Kulturforum combo-ticket—a.k.a. Quartier-Karte, www.kulturforum-berlin.de.

Getting There: Ride the S-Bahn or U-Bahn to Potsdamer Platz, then walk along Potsdamer Platz; from Bahnhof Zoo, you could take bus #200 to Philharmonie (a very slow trip during rush hour).

▲▲Gemäldegalerie

Literally the "Painting Gallery," the Gemäldegalerie is Germany's top collection of 13th- through 18th-century European paintings (more than 1,400 canvases). They're beautifully displayed in a building that's a work of art in itself. The North Wing starts with German paintings of the 13th to 16th century, including eight by Albrecht Dürer. Then come the Dutch and Flemish—Jan van Eyck, Pieter Brueghel, Peter Paul Rubens, Anthony van Dyck, Frans Hals, and Jan Vermeer. The wing finishes with German, English, and French 18th-century artists, such as Thomas Gainsborough and Antoine Watteau. An octagonal hall at the end features an impressive stash of Rembrandts. The South Wing is saved for the Italians—Giotto, Botticelli, Titian, Raphael, and Caravaggio.

Cost and Hours: €10, covered by Kulturforum combo-ticket, Tue-Fri 10:00-18:00, Thu until 20:00, Sat-Sun 11:00-18:00, closed Mon, audioguide included with entry, clever little loaner stools, great salad bar in cafeteria upstairs, Matthäikirchplatz 4, tel. 030/266-424-242, www.smb.museum.

◑ Self-Guided Tour: I'll point out a few highlights, focusing on Northern European artists (German, Dutch, and Flemish), with a few Spaniards and Italians thrown in. To go beyond my selections, make ample use of the excellent audioguide.

The collection spreads out on one vast floor surrounding a central hall. Inner rooms have Roman numerals (I, II, III), while adjacent outer rooms are numbered (1, 2, 3). After showing your ticket, turn right into room I and work your way counterclockwise (and roughly chronologically) through the collection.

Rooms I-III/1-4 kick things off with early German paintings (13th-16th century). In Room 1, look for the 1532 portrait of wealthy Hanseatic cloth merchant Georg Gisze by **Hans Holbein the Younger** (1497-1543). Gisze's name appears on several of the notes stuck to the wall behind him. And, typical of detail-rich Northern European art, the canvas is bursting with highly symbolic tidbits. Items scattered on the tabletop and on the shelves behind the merchant represent his lofty status and aspects of his life story. In the vase, the carnation represents his recent engagement, and the herbs symbolize his virtue.

And yet, the celebratory flowers have already begun to fade and the scales behind him are unbalanced, reminders of the fleetingness of happiness and wealth.

In Room 2 are fine portraits by the remarkably talented **Albrecht Dürer** (1471-1528), who traveled to Italy during the burgeoning days of the early Renaissance and melded the artistic harmony and classical grandeur he discovered there with a Northern European attention to detail. In his *Portrait of Hieronymus Holzschuher* (1526), Dürer skillfully captured the personality of a friend from Nürnberg, right down to the sly twinkle in his sidelong glance. Technically the portrait is perfection: Look closely and see each individual hair of the man's beard and fur coat, and even the reflection of the studio's windows in his eyes. Also notice Dürer's little pyramid-shaped, D-inside-A signature. Signing one's work was a revolutionary assertion of Dürer's renown at a time when German artists were considered anonymous craftsmen.

Lucas Cranach the Elder (1472-1553), whose works are in Room III, was a court painter for the prince electors of Saxony and a close friend of Martin Luther (and his unofficial portraitist). But *The Fountain of Youth* (1546) is a far cry from Cranach's solemn portrayals of the reformer. Old women helped to the fountain (on the left) emerge as young ladies on the right. Newly nubile, the women go into a tent to dress up, snog with noblemen in the bushes (right foreground), dance merrily beneath the trees, and dine grandly beneath a landscape of phallic mountains and towers. This work is flanked by Cranach's Venus nudes. I sense a pattern here.

Dutch painters (Rooms IV-VI/4-7) were early adopters of oil paint (as opposed to older egg tempera)—its relative ease of han-

dling allowed them to brush the super-fine details for which they became famous. **Rogier van der Weyden** (Room IV) was a virtuoso of the new medium. In *Portrait of a Young Woman* (c. 1400-1464), the subject wears a typical winged bonnet, addressing the viewer directly with her fetching blue eyes. The subjects (especially women) of most portraits of the time look off to one side; some art historians guess that the confident woman shown here is Van der Weyden's wife. In the same room is a remarkable, rare trio of three-panel altarpieces by Van der Weyden: The Marienaltar shows the life of the Virgin Mary; the Johannesaltar

narrates the life of John the Baptist—his birth, baptizing Christ (with God and the Holy Spirit hovering overhead), and his gruesome death by decapitation; and the Middelburger Altar tells the story of the Nativity. Savor the fine details in each panel of these altarpieces.

Flash forward a few hundred years to the 17th century and Flemish (Belgian) painting (Rooms VII-VIII/9-10), and it's ap-

parent how much the Protestant Reformation—and resulting Counter-Reformation—changed the tenor of Northern European art. In works by **Peter Paul Rubens** (1577-1640)—including *Jesus Giving Peter the Keys to Heaven*—calm, carefully studied, detail-oriented seriousness gives way to an exuberant Baroque trumpeting of the greatness of the Catholic Church. In the Counter-Reformation world, the Catholic Church had

serious competition for the hearts and minds of its congregants. Exciting art like this became a way to keep people in the pews. Notice the quivering brushstrokes and almost too-bright colors. (In the same room are portraits by Rubens' student, Anthony van Dyck, as well as some hunting still lifes from Frans Snyders and others.) In the next rooms (VIII and 9) are more Rubens, including the mythological *Perseus Freeing Andromeda* and *The Martyrdom of St. Sebastian by Arrows* (loosely based on a more famous rendition by Andrea Mantegna).

Dutch painting from the 17th century (Rooms IX-XI/10-19) is dominated by the convivial portraits by **Frans Hals** (c. 1582-1666). His 1620 portrait of Catharina Hooft (far corner, Room 13) presents a startlingly self-possessed baby (the newest member of a wealthy merchant family) dressed with all the finery of a queen, adorned with lace and jewels, and clutching a golden rattle. The smiling nurse supporting the tyke offers her a piece of fruit, whose blush of red perfectly matches the nanny's apple-fresh cheeks.

But the ultimate Dutch master is **Rembrandt van Rijn** (1606-1669), whose powers of perception and invention propelled him to fame in his lifetime. Displayed here are several storytelling scenes (Room 16), mostly from classical mythology or biblical stories, all employing Rembrandt's trademark chiaroscuro technique (with a strong contrast between light and dark). In *The Rape of Persephone*, Pluto grabs Persephone from his chariot and races toward the underworld, while other goddesses cling to her robe, trying to save her. Cast against a nearly black background, the almost overexposed, action-packed scene is shockingly emotional. In the nearby *Samson and Delilah*

(1628), Delilah cradles Samson's head in her lap while silently signaling to a goon to shear Samson's hair, the secret to his strength. A self-portrait (Room X) of a 28-year-old Rembrandt wearing a beret is paired with the come-hither 1637 *Portrait of Hendrickje Stoffels* (the two were romantically linked). *Samson Threatens His Father-in-Law* (1635) captures the moment just after the mighty

Samson (with his flowing hair, elegant robes, and shaking fist) has been told by his wife's father to take a hike. I wouldn't want to cross this guy.

Although **Johannes Vermeer** (1632-1675) is today just as admired as Rembrandt, he was little known in his day, probably because he painted relatively few works for a small circle of Delft collectors. Vermeer was a master at conveying a complicated story through a deceptively simple scene with a few poignant details—whether it's a woman reading a letter at a window, a milkmaid pouring milk from a pitcher into a bowl, or (as in *The Glass of Wine*, Room 18) a young man offering a drink to a young lady. The young man had been playing her some music on his lute (which now sits, discarded, on a chair) and is hoping to seal the deal with some alcohol. The woman is finishing one glass of wine, and her would-be suitor stands ready—almost *too* ready—to pour her another. His sly, somewhat smarmy smirk drives home his high hopes for what will come next. Vermeer has perfectly captured the exact moment of "Will she or won't she?" The painter offers some clues—the coat of arms in the window depicts a woman holding onto the reins of a horse, staying in control—but ultimately, only he (and the couple) know how this scene will end.

Shift south to Italian, French, and Spanish painting of the 17th and 18th centuries (Rooms XII-XIV/23-28). Venetian cityscapes

by Canaletto (who also painted Dresden) and lots of bombastic Baroque art hang in Room XII. Room XIII features big-name Spanish artists Murillo, Zurbarán, and the great **Diego Velázquez** (1599-1660). He gave the best of his talents to his portraits, capturing warts-and-all likenesses that are effortlessly real. His 1630 *Portrait of a Lady* conveys the subject's subtle, sly Mona Lisa smile. Her figure and face (against a dull gray background) are filtered through a pleasant natural light. Notice that if you stand too close, the brushstrokes get muddy—but when you back up, the scene snaps into perfectly sharp relief.

From here, the collection itself takes a step backwards—into Italian paintings of the 13th-16th century (Rooms XV-XVIII/29-41). This section includes some lesser-known works by great Italian Renaissance painters, including Raphael (Rooms XVII and 29, with five different Madonnas, among them the *Terranuova Madonna*, in a round frame) and Sandro Botticelli (Room VIII).

Museum of Decorative Arts (Kunstgewerbemuseum)

With ho-hum displays covering a thousand years of applied arts—porcelain, fine *Jugendstil* furniture, Art Deco, and reliquaries—this huge space is mostly a low-rent version of London's Victoria and Albert Museum. The exception is its impressive collection of clothing (mostly women's) through the ages, which is worth ▲. It's presented in chronological order and accompanied by bits of historical context that make fashion seem more fascinating than fickle, even to the style-challenged (we know who we are).

Cost and Hours: Covered by Kulturforum combo-ticket, Tue-Fri 10:00-18:00, Sat-Sun 11:00-18:00, closed Mon, Herbert-von-Karajan-Strasse 10, tel. 030/266-424-242, www.smb.museum/kgm.

▲Musical Instruments Museum (Musikinstrumenten Museum)

This striking hall is filled with 600 exhibits spanning the 16th century to modern times. Wander among old keyboard instruments and funny-looking tubas. Pick up the included audioguide and free English brochure at the entry. In addition to the English commentary, the audioguide lets you listen to various instruments being played. This place is fascinating if you're into pianos.

Cost and Hours: €6, covered by Kulturforum combo-ticket, Tue-Fri 9:00-17:00, Thu until 20:00, Sat-Sun 10:00-17:00, closed Mon, low-profile white building east of the big yellow Philharmonic Concert Hall, tel. 030/2548-1178, www.sim.spk-berlin.de.

Philharmonic Concert Hall

Poke into the lobby of Berlin's yellow Philharmonic building and see if there are tickets available during your stay. The interior is famous for its extraordinary acoustics. Even from the outside, this is a remarkable building, designed by a nautical engineer to look like a ship—notice how different it looks from each angle. Inexpensive and legitimate tickets are often sold on the street before performances. Or you can buy tickets from the box office in person, by phone, or online (ticket office open Mon-Fri 15:00-18:00, Sat-Sun 11:00-14:00 except closed July-Aug, tel. 030/2548-8999—answered daily 9:00-18:00, July-Aug until 16:00, www.berliner-philharmoniker.de). For guest performances, you must buy tickets through the organizer (see website for details).

NEAR THE HAUPTBAHNHOF
Natural History Museum (Museum für Naturkunde)

This museum is worth a visit just to see the largest dinosaur skeleton ever assembled. While you're there, meet "Bobby" the stuffed ape, and tour the Wet Collections, displaying shelf after shelf of animals preserved in ethanol (about a million all together). The museum is a magnet for the city's children, who love the interactive displays, the "History of the Universe in 120 Seconds" exhibit, and the cool virtual-reality "Jurascope" glasses that put meat and skin on all the dinosaur skeletons.

Cost and Hours: €6, €3.50 for kids, Tue-Fri 9:30-18:00, Sat-Sun 10:00-18:00, closed Mon, Invalidenstrasse 43, U6: Naturkundemuseum, tel. 030/2093-8591, www.naturkundemuseum-berlin.de.

BERLIN

Sights in Western Berlin

ON AND NEAR KURFÜRSTENDAMM

Western Berlin's main drag, Kurfürstendamm boulevard (nicknamed "Ku'damm," and worth ▲), starts at Kaiser Wilhelm Memorial Church and does a commercial cancan for two miles. In the 1850s, when Berlin became a wealthy and important capital, her "new rich" chose Kurfürstendamm as their street. Bismarck made it Berlin's Champs-Elysées. In the 1920s, it was a stylish and fashionable drag of cafés and boutiques. During the Third Reich, as home to an international community of diplomats and journalists, it enjoyed more freedom than the rest of Berlin. Throughout the Cold War, economic subsidies from the West made sure that capitalism thrived on Ku'damm. Today, while much of the old charm has been hamburgerized, Ku'damm is still a fine place to enjoy elegant shops (around Fasanenstrasse), department stores, and people-watching.

▲Kaiser Wilhelm Memorial Church (Gedächtniskirche)

This church was originally dedicated to the first emperor of Germany, Wilhelm I. Reliefs and mosaics show great events in the life of Germany's favorite *Kaiser*, from his coronation in 1871 to his death in 1888. The church's bombed-out ruins have been left standing as a poignant memorial to the destruction of Berlin in World War II.

Cost and Hours: Church—free, daily 9:00-19:00; Memorial Hall—free, Mon-Fri 10:00-18:00, Sat 10:00-17:30, Sun 12:00-17:30. Located on Breitscheidplatz, U2/U9 and S-Bahn: Zoologischer Garten or U1/U9: Kurfürstendamm, www.gedaechtniskirche-berlin.de.

Visiting the Church: The church is actually an ensemble of buildings: a new church, the matching bell tower, a meeting hall, and the ruins of the old church, with its Memorial Hall. Work is underway to strengthen all four buildings and make it possible to visit the top of the church.

Under a Neo-Romanesque mosaic ceiling, the **Memorial Hall** features a small exhibit of interesting photos about the bombing and before-and-after models of the church. After the war, some Berliners wanted to tear down the ruins and build it anew. Instead, it was decided to keep what was left of the old church as a memorial and stage a competition to design a contemporary, add-on section. The winning entry—the short, modern church (1961) next to the Memorial Hall—offers a meditative world of 11,000 little blue windows. The blue glass was given to the church by the French as a reconciliation gift. For more information on both churches, pick up the English flier.

As you enter the **church,** turn immediately right to find a simple charcoal sketch of the Virgin Mary wrapped in a shawl. During the Battle of Stalingrad, German combat surgeon Kurt Reuber rendered the Virgin on the back of a stolen Soviet map to comfort the men in his care. On the right are the words "Light, Life, Love" from the gospel of John; on the left, "Christmas in the cauldron 1942"; and at the bottom, "Fortress Stalingrad." Though Reuber died in captivity a year later, his sketch was flown out of Stalingrad on the last medical evacuation flight, and postwar Germany embraced it as a symbol of the wish for peace. Copies of the drawing, now known as the *Stalingrad Madonna,* hang in the Berlin Cathedral, in St. Michael's Cathedral in Coventry, England, and in the Kozan Cathedral in Russia's Volgograd (formerly Stalingrad) as a sign of peaceful understanding among nations. As another act of reconciliation, every Friday at 13:00 a "Prayers for Peace" service is held simultaneously here and at the cathedral in Coventry.

Nearby: The lively square between the churches and the Europa Center (a shiny high-rise shopping center built as a showcase of Western capitalism during the Cold War) usually attracts street musicians and performers—especially in the summer. Berliners call the funky fountain the "wet meatball."

The Story of Berlin

Filling most of what seems like a department store space right on Ku'damm (at #207), this sprawling history exhibit tells the stormy 800-year story of Berlin in a creative way. While there are almost no real historic artifacts, the exhibit does a good job of cobbling together many dimensions of the life and tumultuous times of this great city (and almost everything's in English). It's particularly strong on the story of the city from World War I through the Cold War. However, for similar information, and more artifacts, the German History Museum on Unter den Linden is a far better use of your time and money.

Cost and Hours: €12, daily 10:00-20:00, last entry 2 hours before closing, tel. 030/8872-0100, www.story-of-berlin.de. Times for the 30-minute bunker tour are posted at the entry.

▲Käthe Kollwitz Museum

This local artist (1867-1945), who experienced much of Berlin's stormiest century, conveys powerful, deeply felt emotions about motherhood, war, and suffering through the stark faces of her art (she lost her youngest son in World War I). This small yet fine collection (the only one in town of Kollwitz's work) consists of three floors of charcoal drawings and woodcuts, topped by an attic with a handful of sculptures.

Cost and Hours: €6, daily 11:00-18:00, a block off Ku'damm at Fasanenstrasse 24, U-Bahn: Uhlandstrasse, tel. 030/882-5210, www.kaethe-kollwitz.de.

▲Kaufhaus des Westens (KaDeWe)

The "Department Store of the West" has been a Berlin tradition for more than a century. With a staff of 2,100 to help you sort through its vast selection of 380,000 items, KaDeWe claims to be the biggest department store on the Continent. You can get everything from a haircut and train ticket (third floor) to souvenirs (fourth floor). The theater and concert box office on the sixth floor charges an 18 percent booking fee, but they know all your options (cash only). The sixth floor is a world of gourmet taste treats. The biggest selection of deli and exotic food in Germany offers plenty of classy opportunities to sit down and eat. Ride the glass elevator to the seventh floor's glass-domed Winter Garden, a self-service cafeteria—fun but pricey.

Hours: Mon-Thu 10:00-20:00, Fri 10:00-21:00, Sat 9:30-20:00, closed Sun, S-Bahn: Zoologischer Garten or U-Bahn: Wittenbergplatz, tel. 030/21210, www.kadewe.de.

Nearby: The Wittenbergplatz U-Bahn station (in front of KaDeWe) is a unique opportunity to see an old-time station. Enjoy its interior with classic advertisements still decorating its venerable walls.

Berlin Zoo and Aquarium (Zoologischer Garten Berlin)

More than 1,500 different kinds of animals call Berlin's famous zoo home...or so the zookeepers like to think. The big hit here is the lonely panda bear (straight in from the entrance). The adjacent aquarium is world-class.

Cost and Hours: Zoo-€13, aquarium-€13, €20 for both, kids half-price, daily 9:00-18:30, until 17:00 in winter, aquarium closes at 18:00 year-round; feeding times—*Fütterungszeiten*—posted just inside entrance, the best feeding show is the sea lions—generally at 15:15; enter near Europa Center in front of Hotel Palace or opposite Bahnhof Zoo on Hardenbergplatz, Budapester Strasse 34, tel. 030/254-010, www.zoo-berlin.de.

CHARLOTTENBURG PALACE AREA

The Charlottenburg district—with a cluster of museums across the street from a grand palace—is an easy side-trip from downtown. The palace isn't much to see, but if the surrounding museums appeal to you, consider making the trip.

Getting There: Ride U2 to Sophie-Charlotte Platz and walk 10 minutes up the tree-lined boulevard Schlossstrasse (following signs to *Schloss*), or—much faster—catch bus #M45 (direction: Spandau) direct from Bahnhof Zoo or bus #109 from along Ku'damm (direction: Flughafen Tempel).

Eating near Charlottenburg Palace: For lunch, try the traditional German grub at **Brauhaus Lemke** brewpub or sample Russian specialties at **Samowar**.

▲Charlottenburg Palace (Schloss Charlottenburg)

Charlottenburg Palace is the largest former residence of the royal Hohenzollern family in Berlin, and contains the biggest collection of 17th-century French fresco painting outside France. If you've seen the great palaces of Europe, this Baroque palace comes in at about number 10. I'd rate it behind Potsdam, too, though Charlottenburg is arguably a more pleasant outing: It's easy to reach, involves no timed tickets, has good audioguides, and is across the street from a pair of great art museums. In 2016 the central "Old Palace" (Altes Schloss) is closed for renovation; the New Wing (Neue Flügel) remains open.

Cost and Hours: New Wing-€8, more during special exhibitions, includes well-done audioguide, Wed-Mon 10:00-18:00, Nov-March until 17:00, closed Tue, when facing the palace walk toward the right wing, tel. 0331/969-4200, www.spsg.de.

Visiting the Palace: The New Wing (Neue Flügel, a.k.a. the Knobelsdorff Wing) features a few royal apartments and the Golden Gallery, a real-life Cinderella ballroom. Go upstairs and take a substantial hike through restored-since-the-war gold-crusted white rooms. Yes, that *Napoleon Crossing the Alps* painting is the real deal (one of five originals done by Jacques-Louis David). Out back are sprawling gardens (free) with a few royal pavilions that I wouldn't take time to visit (€2-4 each, covered by combo-ticket, fans of Caspar David Friedrich may find the New Pavilion's paintings worthwhile).

▲Museum Berggruen

This tidy little museum is a pleasant surprise, and would be worth ▲▲ in a city with fewer blockbuster sights. Climb three floors through a fun and substantial collection of Picassos. Along the

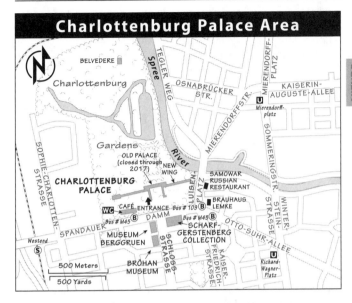

way, you'll see plenty of notable works by Henri Matisse, Paul Klee, and Alberto Giacometti, all accompanied by helpful English descriptions.

Cost and Hours: €10 combo-ticket includes audioguide and Scharf-Gerstenberg Collection, open Tue-Fri 10:00-18:00, Sat-Sun 11:00-18:00, closed Mon, Schlossstrasse 1, tel. 030/266-424-242, www.smb.museum.

▲Scharf-Gerstenberg Collection

This pleasant museum, worth ▲▲ for enthusiasts, houses a collection of more than 250 works of disturbing Surrealist and pre-Surrealist art, thoughtfully organized by theme. The *Surreal Worlds* exhibit shows just how freaky the world looked to artists like Salvador Dalí, Paul Klee, and Francisco de Goya. The grand space connecting the museum's two wings beautifully shows off the huge Kalabsha Gate, salvaged from an ancient Egyptian temple before it was moved to make way for the Aswan Dam.

Cost and Hours: €10 combo-ticket includes audioguide and Museum Berggruen, open Tue-Fri 10:00-18:00, Sat-Sun 11:00-18:00, closed Mon, Schlossstrasse 70, tel. 030/266-424-242, www.smb.museum.

Bröhan Museum

Wander through a dozen *Jugendstil* and Art Deco living rooms, a curvy organic world of lamps, glass, silver, and posters. English descriptions are posted on the wall of each room on the main floor.

While you're there, look for the fine collection of Impressionist paintings by Karl Hagemeister.

Cost and Hours: €8, more with special exhibits, Tue-Sun 10:00-18:00, closed Mon, Schlossstrasse 1A, tel. 030/3269-0600, www.broehan-museum.de.

Shopping in Berlin

Berlin Story, a big, cluttered, fun bookshop (not to be confused with the Story of Berlin museum on Ku'damm), has a knowledge-able staff and the best selection anywhere in town of English-language books and helpful magazines on Berlin. They also stock an amusing mix of knickknacks and East Berlin nostalgia souvenirs (Mon-Sat 10:00-19:00, Sun 10:00-18:00, Unter den Linden 40, tel. 030/2045-3842).

If you're taken with the city's unofficial mascot, the Am-pelmännchen (traffic-light man), you'll find a world of souvenirs slathered with his iconic red and green image at **Ampelmann Shops** (several locations, including along Unter den Linden at #35, near Gendarmenmarkt at Markgrafenstrasse 37, near Museum Island inside the DomAquarée mall, in the Hackesche Höfe, and at Potsdamer Platz).

Fun and funky **designer shops** fill the Hackesche Höfe and are easy to find throughout Prenzlauer Berg, particularly along Kastanienallee and Oderberger Strasse. In Kreuzberg, head to Bergmannstrasse for designer boutiques and plenty of antiques (U-Bahn: Gneisenaustrasse).

Flea markets abound in Berlin, and virtually every neighbor-hood hosts one on a regular basis. The most central is along Am Kupfergraben, just across the canal from the Pergamon and Bode museums, with lots of books, music, and art (Sat-Sun 10:00-17:00). One of the biggest is right next to the Tiergarten park on Strasse des 17 Juni, with great antiques, more than 200 stalls, collector-savvy merchants, and fun German fast-food stands (Sat-Sun 6:00-16:00, S-Bahn: Tiergarten). The rummage market in Prenzlauer Berg's Mauerpark comes with lots of inventive snack stalls—and on Sunday afternoons, karaoke in the park's amphitheater (Sat-Sun 7:00-17:00, U-Bahn: Eberswalder Strasse). And on Sunday morn-ings the north side of the Ostbahnhof is the place to pick among the Cold War knickknacks that keep turning up in the basements of former East Berliners.

On the opposite end of the price spectrum are the swanky shopping centers clustered around **Gendarmenmarkt** and the glitzy luxury shops along **Ku'damm**—the place to go if you're in the market for another Rolls Royce. Nearby is **KaDeWe**, one of Europe's fanciest department stores, with a good selection of souvenirs...and just about anything else you can think of. Near the Bahnhof Zoo train station is the popular new **Bikinihaus** shopping center—a "concept mall" full of local artisan boutiques. Farther west, the Charlottenburg neighborhood's **"Antique Mile"** stretches along Suarezstrasse (between Kanstrasse and the Sophie-Charlotte Platz U-Bahn stop).

Weekly **farmers markets** are huge in this city of foodies, and the biggest include stalls proffering fresh snacks of all kinds. A local favorite is on Baxhagener Platz in quickly gentrifying Friedrichshain, east of Prenzlauer Berg (Sat 8:00-14:30, U-Bahn: Samariterstrasse). More central is the twice weekly market that fills Hackescher Markt on Thursdays (bigger, 9:00-18:00) and Saturdays (10:00-18:00).

Nightlife in Berlin

Berlin is a happening place for nightlife—whether it's clubs, pubs, jazz music, cabaret, hokey-but-fun German variety shows, theater, or concerts.

Entertainment Info: *Berlin Programm* lists a nonstop parade of concerts, plays, exhibits, and cultural events (€2.20, in German, www.berlinprogramm.de); *Exberliner Magazine* (€3, www.exberliner.com) doesn't have as much hard information, but is colorfully written in English (sold at kiosks). For the young and determined sophisticate, *Zitty* and *Tip* are the top guides to alternative culture (mostly in German, sold at kiosks). Also pick up the free schedules *Flyer* and *030* in bars and clubs. Visit KaDeWe's ticket office for your music and theater options (sixth floor, 18 percent fee but access to all tickets). Ask about "competitive improvisation" and variety shows.

Half-Price Tickets: Hekticket, Berlin's ticket clearinghouse, is good for whatever's happening in town. They offer regular tickets in advance and same-day half-price tickets to concerts, cabaret, theater, and so on. Drop by or call after 14:00 to see what's on the push list for this evening—ticket prices usually range from €10 to €40 (Mon-Fri 12:00-18:00, closed Sat-Sun, half-price sales start at 14:00, near Alexanderplatz at Karl-Liebknecht-Strasse 13, tel. 030/230-9930, www.hekticket.de). They also have a branch in western Berlin (Mon-Sat 12:00-20:00, Sun 14:00-18:00, across from Bahnhof Zoo at Hardenbergstrasse 29).

Berlin Jazz

To enjoy live music near my recommended Savignyplatz hotels in western Berlin, consider **A Trane Jazz Club** (all jazz, great stage and intimate seating, €10-25 cover depending on act, opens at 20:00, live music nightly from 21:00, Bleibtreustrasse 1, tel. 030/313-

2550, www.a-trane.de). **B-Flat Acoustic Music and Jazz Club,** in the heart of eastern Berlin, also has live music nightly—and shares a courtyard with a tranquil tea house (shows vary from free to €10-13 cover, open Sun-Thu from 20:00 with shows starting at 21:00, Fri-Sat from 21:00 with shows at 22:00, a block from Rosenthaler Platz U-Bahn stop at Rosenthaler Strasse 13, tel. 030/283-3123, www.b-flat-berlin.de).

Berliner Rock and Roll

Berlin has a vibrant rock and pop scene, with popular venues at the Spandau Citadel, Olympic Stadium, and the outdoor Waldbühne ("Forest Stage"). Check out what's playing on posters in the U-Bahn, in *Zitty,* or at any ticket agency.

Cabaret

Bar Jeder Vernunft offers modern-day cabaret a short walk from my recommended hotels in western Berlin. This variety show—under a classic old tent perched atop the modern parking lot of the Berliner Festspiele theater—is a hit with German speakers, and can be worthwhile for those who don't speak the language (as some of the music shows are in a sort of *Deutsch*-English hybrid). Some Americans even perform here periodically. Tickets run about €22-30, and shows change regularly (performances generally Tue-Sat at 20:00, Sun at 19:00, seating can be cramped, south of Ku'damm at Schaperstrasse 24, U3 or U9: Spichernstrasse, tel. 030/883-1582, www.bar-jeder-vernunft.de).

Nightclubs and Pubs

Oranienburger Strasse is a trendy scene, with bars and restaurants spilling out onto sidewalks filled with people strolling. To the north, you'll find the hip **Prenzlauer Berg** neighborhood, packed with everything from smoky pubs to small art bars and dance clubs (best scene is around Helmholtzplatz, U2: Eberswalder Strasse).

These days, the most happening scene is generally a few more tram stops or U-Bahn stops out from the center, in the neighborhoods of Friedrichshain (just east of Prenzlauer Berg) and Neukölln (immediately south of Kreuzberg). One particularly inviting venue is **Radialsystem,** a building right by the water and near the East Side Gallery, hosting a variety of events and concerts—everything from classical to electronic (and good €5 meals to boot, Holzmarktstrasse 33, take S-Bahn to Ostbahnhof station, www.radialsystem.de). The edgier **RAW-Tempel,** just north of the Warschauerstrasse S-Bahn station, is a huge complex of industrial buildings that have been renovated by a community group dedicated to hosting low-cost arts events, including club nights, concerts, a bar, and even a circus (www.raw-tempel.de).

Dancing

Dance up a storm at **Clärchens Ballhaus,** an old ballroom that's been a Berlin institution since 1913. At some point everyone in Berlin comes through here, as the dance hall attracts an eclectic Berlin-in-a-nutshell crowd of grannies, elegant women in evening dresses, yuppies, scenesters, and hippies. The music (swing, waltz, tango, or cha-cha) changes every day, with live music on Friday and Saturday (from 23:15, €5 cover; dance hall open daily from 11:00—12:00 in winter—until the last person goes home, in the heart of the Auguststrasse gallery district at Auguststrasse 24, S-Bahn: Oranienburger Strasse, tel. 030/282-9295, www.ballhaus. de). Dancing lessons are also available (€9, beginners' lessons Thu at 19:30 and Sun at 12:00, 1.5 hours). The Gipsy Restaurant, which fills a huge courtyard out front, serves reasonably priced German and Italian food.

Berlin boasts the largest **tango** scene outside Buenos Aires, and in summer it's on display on any balmy night in Monbijou Park, the pleasant riverside green space between Museum Island and Hackescher Markt. Most nights also include sessions with one or two other dance styles (€6 beginners' classes often available; www.monbijou-theater.de).

Late-Hours Sightseeing

Berlin's museums typically close at 18:00, but many stay open later at least one day a week, allowing smart planners to stretch their sightseeing day. Four of the biggies are open late every day: the Reichstag (until midnight, last entry at 22:00), the Museum of the Wall at Checkpoint Charlie (until 22:00), the Topography of Terror (until 20:00), and the Jewish Museum Berlin (Tue-Sun until 20:00, 22:00 on Mon). All of the Museum Island museums are open until 20:00 on Thursdays.

Outdoor monuments such as the Berlin Wall Memorial and the Memorial to the Murdered Jews of Europe are accessible, safe, and pleasantly lit late into the night, though their visitor centers close earlier. Many of Berlin's art galleries are also open late (see next)—consider an evening gallery stroll.

Art Galleries

Berlin, a magnet for new artists, is a great city for gallery visits. Galleries—many of which stay open late—welcome visitors who are "just looking." The most famous gallery district is in eastern Berlin's Mitte neighborhood, along **Auguststrasse** (branches off from Oranienburger Strasse). Check out the Berlin outpost of the edgy-yet-accessible art of the New Leipzig movement at **Galerie Eigen+Art** (Tue-Sat 11:00-18:00, closed Sun-Mon, Auguststrasse 26, tel. 030/280-6605, www.eigen-art.com). The other gallery area is in western Berlin, along **Fasanenstrasse.**

BERLIN

Pub Crawls

The "free" tour companies that cater to students offer wildly popular pub crawls, promising "four cool bars and one hot club" for about €12. Just imagine what kind of bar lets in a tour of 70 college kids. It can be fun...if you want to get drunk with a bunch of American students in a foreign country.

Sleeping in Berlin

Berlin is packed and hotel prices go up on holidays, including Green Week in mid-January, Easter weekend, the first weekend in May, Ascension weekend in May, German Unity Day (Oct 3), Christmas, and New Year's.

IN EASTERN BERLIN
Prenzlauer Berg

Gentrification has brought the colorful and gritty Prenzlauer Berg district great hotels, tasty ethnic and German eateries, and a happening nightlife scene. Think of all the graffiti as just some people's way of saying they care. The huge and impersonal concrete buildings are enlivened by their ground-level street fair of fun little shops and eateries.

This loosely defined area is about 1.5 miles north of Alexanderplatz, roughly between Kollwitzplatz and Helmholtzplatz, and to the west, along Kastanienallee (known affectionately as "Casting Alley" for its generous share of beautiful people). The closest U-Bahn stops are U2: Senefelderplatz at the south end of the neighborhood, U8: Rosenthaler Platz in the middle, or U2: Eberswalder Strasse at the north end. Or, for less walking, take the S-Bahn to Hackescher Markt, then catch tram #M1 north.

$$$ Myer's Hotel rents 60 lush rooms decorated in rich colors with classy furnishings. The gorgeous public spaces, including an art-filled patio and garden, host frequent cultural events. This peaceful hub—off a quiet garden courtyard and tree-lined street—makes it hard to believe you're in a capital city (Sb-€80-195, Db-€108-235, price depends on season and size—check rates online, air-con, elevator, sauna, bike rental-€10/day, Metzer Strasse 26, 5-minute walk to Kollwitzplatz or U2: Senefelderplatz, tel. 030/440-140, www.myershotel.de, info@myershotel.de).

$$$ Hotel Jurine (zhoo-REEN—the family name) is a pleasant 53-room business-style hotel whose friendly staff aims to please. In good weather, you can enjoy the breakfast buffet on the peaceful backyard patio and garden (Sb-€90-110, Db-€130-160, extra bed-€35, rates vary by season, check website for discounts July-Aug, mention this book and book direct for courtyard-facing room at no extra charge if available, air-con only on upper floor, elevator,

---

Sleep Code

Abbreviations   (€1=about $1.10, country code: 49)
S=Single, **D**=Double/Twin, **T**=Triple, **Q**=Quad, **b**=bathroom
Price Rankings
  $$$ **Higher Priced**—Most rooms €125 or more
    $$ **Moderately Priced**—Most rooms €85-125
      $ **Lower Priced**—Most rooms €85 or less
Unless otherwise noted, credit cards are accepted, breakfast
is included, free Wi-Fi and/or a guest computer is generally
available, and English is spoken. Berlin hotels must charge a
5 percent tax, which may not be included in the prices listed
here. Prices change; verify current rates online or by email. For
the best prices, always book directly with the hotel.

---

garage parking-€13.50/day—reserve ahead, Schwedter Strasse 15,
10-minute walk to U2: Senefelderplatz, tel. 030/443-2990, www.
hotel-jurine.de, mail@hotel-jurine.de).

$$$ Hotel Kastanienhof feels less urban-classy and more like
a traditional small-town German hotel. It's wonderfully located on
the Kastanienallee #M1 tram line, with easy access to the Pren-
zlauer Berg bustle (but since trams run all night, you may want to
ask for a room on the back). Its 50 rooms come with helpful ser-
vice (Sb-€75-125, Db-€100-180, prices vary widely with demand,
€10/person more for nicely modernized top-floor rooms with air-
con and/or balcony—request when you book direct via email or
phone, extra bed-€20, breakfast-€9, wheelchair-accessible room,
parking-€9/day, 20 yards from #M1 Zionskirche tram stop at Kas-
tanienallee 65, tel. 030/443-050, www.kastanienhof.biz, info@
kastanienhof.biz).

$$ The Circus Hotel is fun, entirely comfortable, and an excellent value. Each of its 60 colorful, trendy rooms has a unique
bit of decoration. It overlooks a busy intersection, so there's some
nighttime noise—ask for a quieter back room. Run by the same
folks who manage the popular Circus Hostel (listed later), it's ser-
vice-oriented, with lots of included extras, a very "green" attitude,
and occasional special events for guests (Sb-€75, small standard
Db-€95, larger Db-€105, junior suite Db-€120, breakfast-€9,
elevator, loaner iPads in rooms, mellow ground-floor restaurant,
Rosenthaler Strasse 1, directly at U8: Rosenthaler Platz, tel.
030/2000-3939, www.circus-berlin.de, info@circus-berlin.de). The
Circus also offers a range of spacious, modern **apartments** both
within the hotel and two blocks away on Choriner Strasse (Db-
€130-€250, 3-night minimum stay preferred).

$ Karlito Apartmenthaus offers 12 well-located, modern,
and comfortable apartments above a hip café on a tranquil side

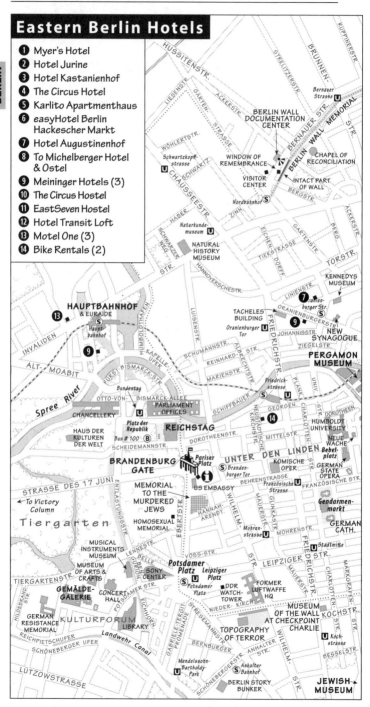

Eastern Berlin Hotels

1. Myer's Hotel
2. Hotel Jurine
3. Hotel Kastanienhof
4. The Circus Hotel
5. Karlito Apartmenthaus
6. easyHotel Berlin Hackescher Markt
7. Hotel Augustinenhof
8. To Michelberger Hotel & Ostel
9. Meininger Hotels (3)
10. The Circus Hostel
11. EastSeven Hostel
12. Hotel Transit Loft
13. Motel One (3)
14. Bike Rentals (2)

BERLIN

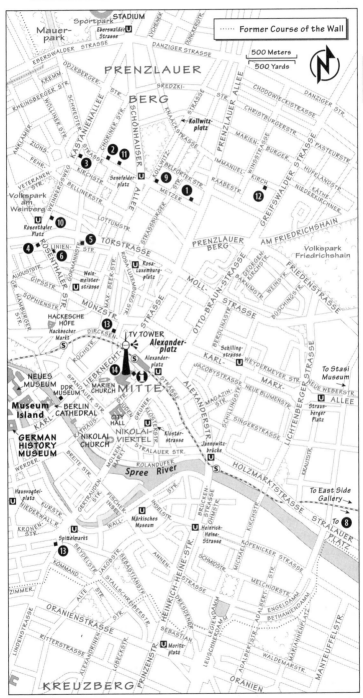

...... Former Course of the Wall

street near Hackescher Markt. All of the sleek, Ikea-esque units have miniature balconies and are fully equipped (Sb-€65-80, Db-€80-95, price depends on season, extra person-€15, up to 2 children under 8 sleep free with 2 paying adults, breakfast served in your room-€10, no minimum stay, elevator, bike rental-€8/day, Linienstrasse 60—check in at Café Lois around the corner on Gormannstrasse, 350 yards from S-Bahn: Hackescher Markt, even closer to U8: Rosenthaler Platz, mobile 0179-704-9041, www.karlito-apartments.de, info@karlito-apartments.de).

$ **easyHotel Berlin Hackescher Markt** is part of an unapologetically cheap Europe-wide chain where you pay for exactly what you use—nothing more, nothing less. Based on parent company easyJet's business model of nickel-and-dime air travel, the hotel has inexpensive base rates (Db-€35-65; prices vary by season and room size, usually cheaper the earlier you book), then charges you separate, sometimes pricey fees for optional extras (Wi-Fi, TV, and so on). The 125 orange-and-gray rooms are very small, basic, and feel popped out of a plastic mold, but if you skip the extras, the price is right, and the location—at the Hackescher Markt end of Prenzlauer Berg—is wonderful (elevator, after booking online call to request a quieter back room, Rosenthaler Strasse 69, tel. 030/4000-6550, www.easyhotel.com).

Near Oranienburger Strasse: $$$ **Hotel Augustinenhof** is a clean hotel with 66 spacious rooms, nice woody floors, and some of the most comfortable beds in Berlin. While not exactly in Prenzlauer Berg, the hotel is on a side street near all the Oranienburger Strasse action. Rooms in front overlook the courtyard of the old Imperial Post Office, rooms in back are a bit quieter, and some rooms have older, thin windows (prices vary with demand, but you'll likely pay around Sb-€80-120 or Db-€100-150, elevator, Auguststrasse 82, 50 yards from S-Bahn: Oranienburger Strasse, tel. 030/3088-6710, www.hotel-augustinenhof.de, augustinenhof@albrechtshof-hotels.de).

Farther East, in Friedrichshain

$$ **Michelberger Hotel,** in the heart of gritty, quickly gentrifying Friedrichshain, is so over-the-top artsy and self-consciously hip that it'd all be just too much...if it weren't for its extremely helpful and friendly staff. Its 113 bright rooms are reasonably priced, and its common spaces—a bar/lounge and a breezy courtyard restaurant—are genuinely welcoming (small Sb/Db-€80-90, bigger "loft" Db-€90-115, Tb-€115-135, Qb-€180-210, suites available, prices vary with demand, €10-20 more for refundable reservation, €16 full breakfast or cheaper à la carte options, elevator, bike rental-€10/day; from atop Warschauer Strasse S-Bahn station turn left to cross the bridge—it's across from the U-Bahn station and #M10

tram stop at Warschauer Strasse 39; tel. 030/2977-8590, www.
michelbergerhotel.com, reservations@michelbergerhotel.com).

$ Ostel is a fun, retro-1970s-DDR apartment building that
re-creates the lifestyle and interior design of a country relegated to
the dustbin of history. All the furniture and room decorations have
been meticulously collected and restored to their former socialist
glory—only the psychedelic wallpaper is a replica. Kitschy, sure—
but also clean and memorable (S-€30, Sb-€36, D-€54, Db-€59,
4-person apartments-€120; about €10 more on weekends, cheaper
off-season; no breakfast but supermarket next door and shops in
nearby train station, 24-hour reception, Wi-Fi in lobby, bike rental, free parking, free collective use of the people's barbeque, right
behind Ostbahnhof station on the corner of Strasse der Pariser
Kommune at Wriezener Karree 5, tel. 030/2576-8660, www.ostel.
eu, contact@ostel.eu).

Hostels in Eastern Berlin

Berlin is known among budget travelers for its fun, hip hostels.
These range from upscale-feeling, with some hotelesque private
rooms comfortable enough even for non-hostelers, to more truly
backpacker-type places where comfort is secondary to socializing.
These are scattered around eastern Berlin, including some (Circus,
Meininger, and EastSeven) in Prenzlauer Berg.

Comfortable Hostels with Hotelesque Rooms

$$ Meininger is a Europe-wide budget-hotel chain with several
locations in Berlin. With sleek, nicely decorated rooms, these can
be a great-value budget option, even for non-hostelers. They have
three particularly appealing branches: in Prenzlauer Berg (Schön-
hauser Allee 19 on Senefelderplatz), at Oranienburger Strasse 67
(next to the Aufsturz pub), and near the Hauptbahnhof, at Ella-
Traebe-Strasse 9 (bunk in dorm room-€20-40, Sb-€50-100,
Db-€70-120, Tb-€60-135; rates vary widely with demand, gen-
erally pricier Fri-Sat, cheaper on Sun; all locations: breakfast-€7,
elevator, 24-hour reception, pay guest computer, guest kitchen,
bike rental-€12/day, pay parking, tel. 030/666-36100, welcome@
meininger-hostels.com, www.meininger-hostels.com).

$ The Circus Hostel is a brightly colored, well-run place with
230 beds, a trendy lounge with upscale ambience, and a bar down-
stairs. It has typical hostel dorms as well as some very hotel-like
private rooms; for a few big steps up in comfort, see the listing
for the Circus Hotel, earlier (bunk in dorm room-€23-31, S-€50,
Sb-€60, D-€66, Db-€85, 2-person kitchenette apartment-€100,
4-person apartment-€160, breakfast-€4-8, no curfew, elevator,
guest iPads, bike rental, Weinbergsweg 1A, U8: Rosenthaler Platz,
tel. 030/2000-3939, www.circus-berlin.de, info@circus-berlin.de).

$ EastSeven Hostel rents the best cheap beds in Prenzlauer Berg. It's sleek and modern, with all the hostel services and more: 60 beds, inviting lounge, fully equipped guest kitchen, lockers, quiet backyard terrace, and bike rental. Children are welcome. Easygoing people of any age are comfortable here (bunk in dorm room-€15-25, S-€35—only available in off-season, D-€54-60, T-€54-70, cheapest on Sun, priciest on Fri-Sat, includes sheets, towel-€1, continental breakfast-€3, laundry-€7, no curfew, 100 yards from U2: Senefelderplatz at Schwedter Strasse 7, tel. 030/9362-2240, www.eastseven.de, info@eastseven.de).

$ Hotel Transit Loft, actually more of a hostel, is located in a refurbished factory. Its 81 stark, high-ceilinged rooms and wide-open lobby have an industrial touch. The reception—staffed by friendly, hip Berliners—is open 24 hours, with a bar serving drinks all night long (Sb-€63, Db-€73, Tb-€94, Qb-€104, Quint/b-€115, includes sheets and breakfast, elevator, fully wheelchair-accessible, down alley facing inner courtyard at Immanuelkirchstrasse 14A; U2/U5/U8 or S-Bahn: Alexanderplatz, then tram #M4 to Hufelandstrasse and walk 50 yards; tel. 030/4849-3773, www.transit-loft.de, loft@hotel-transit.de).

IN WESTERN BERLIN

While western Berlin still works well as a comfortable and handy home base, it's no longer the obvious place from which to explore the city. The area went through an identity crisis when the new Hauptbahnhof essentially put Bahnhof Zoo out of business in 2006. Now, the west side is back, but more as a suburb than the nerve center of the city.

Near Savignyplatz and Bahnhof Zoo

The streets around the tree-lined Savignyplatz have a neighborhood charm, with an abundance of simple, small, friendly, good-value places to sleep and eat. The area has an artsy aura going back to the cabaret days in the 1920s, when it was the center of Berlin's gay scene.

The hotels and pensions I list here—which are all a 5- to 15-minute walk from Bahnhof Zoo and Savignyplatz (with S- and U-Bahn stations)—are generally located a couple of flights up in big, run-down buildings. Inside, they're clean and spacious enough so that their well-worn character is actually charming. Of the accommodations listed here, Pension Peters offers the best value for budget travelers.

$$ Hecker's Hotel is a modern, four-star hotel with 69 big, fresh rooms and all the Euro-comforts. Their "superior" rooms cost €10 more than their "comfort" rooms, and—while the same size—have more modern furnishings and air-conditioning. Herr Kiesel promises free breakfasts (otherwise €16/person) for Rick Steves readers who book direct via the hotel's website or email, plus show a current edition of this book at check-in (Sb-€85, Db-usually €95-100—though all rooms €160 during conferences, look for deals on their website, a few rooms with kitchenettes—ask, elevator, parking-€14-20/day, between Savignyplatz and Ku'damm at Grolmanstrasse 35, tel. 030/88900, www.heckers-hotel.com, info@heckers-hotel.com).

$$ Hotel Carmer 16, with 49 bright and airy (if a bit dated) rooms, is both business-like and homey (Sb-€89, Db-€125, extra person-€30, €10/person less without breakfast, some rooms have balconies, family suites, elevator and a few stairs, pay Wi-Fi, parking-€9.50/day, Carmerstrasse 16, tel. 030/3110-0500, www.hotel-carmer16.de, info@hotel-carmer16.de).

$$ Hotel-Pension Funk, the former home of a 1920s silent-movie star, is a delightfully quirky only-in-Berlin time warp. Kind manager Herr Michael Pfundt offers 15 elegant old rooms with rich Art Nouveau furnishings and hardly any modern trappings, including TVs (S-€45, S with shower but toilet down the hall-€65, Sb-€75, D-€75, D with shower but toilet down the hall-€89, Db-€99, extra person-€25, these prices only when you book direct, cash preferred, a long block south of Ku'damm at Fasanenstrasse 69, tel. 030/882-7193, www.hotel-pensionfunk.de, berlin@hotel-pensionfunk.de).

$ Pension Peters, run by a German-Swedish couple, is sunny and central, with a cheery breakfast room and a super-friendly staff who go out of their way to help their guests. With its sleek Scandinavian decor and 33 renovated rooms, it's a good choice. Some of the ground-floor rooms facing the back courtyard are a bit dark—and cheaper. Annika and Christoph (with help from his sister, Daisy, as well as friendly Uwe and others) have been welcoming my readers for decades, and offer the following special prices with this book and cash in 2016—be sure to book direct and mention this offer when you reserve (Sb-€59, Db-€76, extra bed-€15, family room-€85, breakfast-€6.50, up to 2 kids under 10 free with 2 paying adults, cash preferred, good organic breakfast, bike rental, 10 yards off Savignyplatz at Kantstrasse 146, tel. 030/312-2278, www.pension-peters-berlin.de, info@pension-peters-berlin.de).

ACROSS THE CITY

$ Motel One has eight locations across Berlin; all have the same aqua-and-brown decor and posh-feeling but small rooms. The four most convenient locations in Berlin are right on Alexanderplatz (Dircksenstrasse 36, tel. 030/2005-4080, berlin-alexanderplatz@motel-one.com); near the Bahnhof Zoo (Kantstrasse 10, tel.

BERLIN

Western Berlin Hotels & Restaurants

1 Hecker's Hotel
2 Hotel Carmer 16
3 Hotel-Pension Funk
4 Pension Peters
5 Motel One Berlin-Ku'damm
6 Restaurant Marjellchen
7 Rest. Leibniz-Klause
8 Dicke Wirtin Pub
9 To Weyers Restaurant
10 Café Literaturhaus
11 Die Zwölf Apostel Rest.
12 Zillemarkt Restaurant
13 Ullrich Supermarkt
14 Schleusenkrug Beer Garden
15 Winter Garden Buffet
16 A Trane Jazz Club
17 Bar Jeder Vernunft
18 Fat Tire Bikes

030/3151-7360, berlin-kudamm@motel-one.com); just behind the Hauptbahnhof (Invalidenstrasse 54, tel. 030/3641-0050, berlin-hauptbahnhof@motel-one.com); and a few blocks east of Gendarmenmarkt (Leipziger Strasse 50, U2: Spittelmarkt, tel. 030/2014-3630, berlin-spittelmarkt@motel-one.com). These four tend to charge the same prices (Sb-€69, Db-€84); the less central locations are about €10 less (all are €20-50 more during events, breakfast-€9.50, air-con, guest iPad at front desk, elevator, limited parking-€10-15/day, www.motel-one.com).

Eating in Berlin

There's a world of restaurants to choose from in this ever-changing city. Your best approach may be to just browse the neighborhood you're in until you find something that strikes your fancy, rather than seeking out a particular restaurant. Lunches are especially easy, as the city is crammed with places selling fresh, affordable sandwiches and salads.

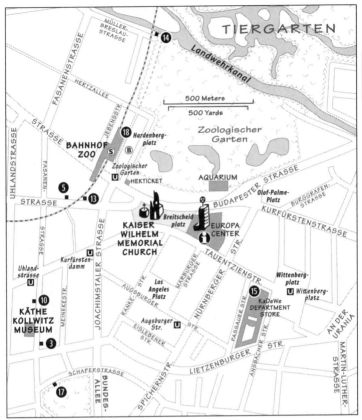

Don't be too determined to eat "Berlin-style." The city is known only for its mildly spicy sausage and for its street food (*Currywurst* and *Döner Kebab*—see the "Berliner Street Fare" sidebar). Germans—especially Berliners—consider their food old-school; when they go out to eat, they're not usually looking for the "traditional local fare" many travelers are after. Nouveau German is California cuisine with scant memories of wurst, kraut, and pumpernickel. If the kraut is getting the wurst of you, take a break with some international or ethnic offerings—try one of the many Turkish, Italian, pan-Asian, and Balkan restaurants.

Colorful pubs—called *Kneipen*—offer light, quick, and easy meals and the fizzy local beer, *Berliner Weiss*. Ask for it *mit Schuss* for a shot of fruity syrup in your suds.

IN EASTERN BERLIN
Near Unter den Linden

While this government/commercial area is hardly a hotspot for

BERLIN

Berliner Street Fare

In Berlin, it's easy to eat cheap, with a glut of *Imbiss* snack stands, bakeries (for sandwiches), and falafel/kebab counters. Train stations have grocery stores, as well as bright and modern fruit-and-sandwich bars.

Sausage stands are everywhere (I've listed the reigning local favorite). Most specialize in **Currywurst**, created in Berlin after World War II, when a fast-food cook got her hands on some curry and Worcestershire sauce from British troops stationed here. It's basically a grilled pork sausage smothered with curry sauce. *Currywurst* comes either *mit Darm* (with casing) or *ohne Darm* (without casing). If the casing is left on to grill, it gives the sausage a smokier flavor. (*Berliner Art*—"Berlin-style"—means that the sausage is boiled *ohne Darm,* then grilled.) Either way, the grilled sausage is then chopped into small pieces or cut in half (East Berlin style) and topped with sauce. While some places simply use ketchup and sprinkle on some curry powder, real *Currywurst* joints use tomato paste, Worcestershire sauce, and curry. With your wurst comes either a toothpick or small wooden fork; you'll usually get a plate of fries as well, but rarely a roll. You'll see *Currywurst* on the menu at some sit-down restaurants, but local purists say that misses the whole point: You'll pay triple and get a less authentic dish than you would at a street stand under elevated S-Bahn tracks.

Other good street foods to consider are *Döner Kebab* (Turkish-style skewered meat slow-roasted and served in a sandwich) and *Frikadelle* (like a hamburger patty; often called *Bulette* in Berlin).

For something quick, cheap, and tasty, find one of the portable human hot-dog stands. Two companies, Grillrunner and Grillwalker, outfit their cooks in clever harnesses that let them grill and sell hot dogs from under an umbrella.

---

eateries, I've listed a few places handy for your sightseeing, all a short walk from Unter den Linden.

Near Museum Island: Georgenstrasse, a block behind the Pergamon Museum and under the S-Bahn tracks, is lined with fun eateries filling the arcade of the train trestle—close to the sightseeing action but in business mainly for students from nearby Humboldt University. **Deponie3** is a reliable Berlin *Kneipe* usually filled with students. Garden seating in the back is nice if you don't mind the noise of the S-Bahn passing directly above you. The interior is a cozy, wooden wonderland of a bar with several inviting spaces.

They serve basic salads, traditional Berlin dishes, and hearty daily specials (€5-8 breakfasts, €10-15 lunches and dinners, daily from 10:00, under S-Bahn arch #187 at Georgenstrasse 5, tel. 030/2016-5740). For Italian food, a branch of **Die Zwölf Apostel** is nearby (food served until 23:00).

Near the TV Tower: **Käse König am Alex** is a wonderfully old-school eatery that's been serving traditional sauerkraut-type dishes since 1933 to hungry locals (with Prussian forks, flat to fit better into a soldier's mess kit). It's fast, the photo menu makes ordering fun, prices are great, and the waitresses are surly (€6-10 dinner plates, daily, Panoramastrasse 1 under the TV Tower, tel. 030/8561-5220). Nearby, **Brauhaus Mitte** is a fun, tour-group-friendly DDR-era beer hall that makes its own beer and offers a menu of Berliner "specialties" and Bavarian dishes. They have decent salads and serve a four-beer sampler board (daily 11:00-24:00, across from the TV Tower at Karl-Liebknecht-Strasse 13, tel. 030/3087-8989).

In the Heart of Old Berlin's Nikolai Quarter: The *Nikolaiviertel* marks the original medieval settlement of Cölln, which would eventually become Berlin. The area was destroyed during the war but was rebuilt for Berlin's 750th birthday in 1987. The whole area has a cute, cobbled, and characteristic old town feel...Middle Ages meets Socialist Realism. Today, the district is pretty soulless by day but a popular restaurant zone at night. **Brauhaus Georgbräu** is a thriving beer hall serving homemade suds on a picturesque courtyard overlooking the Spree River. Eat in the lively and woody but mod-feeling interior, or outdoors with fun riverside seating—thriving with German tourists. It's a good place to try one of the few typical Berlin dishes: *Eisbein* (boiled ham hock) with sauerkraut and mashed peas with bacon (€11 with a beer and schnapps). The statue of St. George once stood in the courtyard of Berlin's old castle—until the Nazis deemed it too decadent and not "German" enough, and removed it (€7-14 plates, daily 12:00-24:00, 2 blocks south of Berlin Cathedral and across the river at Spreeufer 4, tel. 030/242-4244).

Near Gendarmenmarkt

South of Unter den Linden, the twin churches of Gendarmenmarkt seem to be surrounded by people in love with food. The lunch and dinner scene is thriving with upscale restaurants serving good cuisine at highly competitive prices to local professionals. If in need of a quick-yet-classy lunch, stroll around the square and along Charlottenstrasse. For a quick bite, head to the cheap *Currywurst* stand behind the German Cathedral.

Lutter & Wegner Restaurant is well-known for its Austrian cuisine (*Schnitzel* and *Sauerbraten*) and popular with businesspeo-

BERLIN

Eastern Berlin Eateries & Nightlife

1. Deponie3 Pub
2. Die Zwölf Apostel
3. Käse König am Alex
4. Brauhaus Mitte & Hekticket Half-Price Tix
5. Brauhaus Georgbräu
6. Lutter & Wegner Rest.; Augustiner am Gendarmenmarkt
7. Galeries Lafayette Food Circus
8. Hasir Turkish Restaurant
9. Weihenstephaner Bavarian Restaurant
10. Oranienburger Strasse Eateries
11. Schwarzwaldstuben Pub
12. Gipsy Restaurant & Clärchens Ballhaus
13. My Smart Break & Transit Restaurant

BERLIN

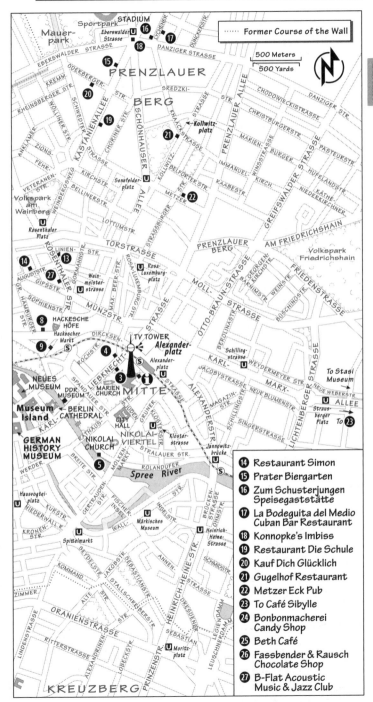

...... Former Course of the Wall

500 Meters
500 Yards

⑭ Restaurant Simon
⑮ Prater Biergarten
⑯ Zum Schusterjungen Speisegaststätte
⑰ La Bodeguita del Medio Cuban Bar Restaurant
⑱ Konnopke's Imbiss
⑲ Restaurant Die Schule
⑳ Kauf Dich Glücklich
㉑ Gugelhof Restaurant
㉒ Metzer Eck Pub
㉓ To Café Sibylle
㉔ Bonbonmacherei Candy Shop
㉕ Beth Café
㉖ Fassbender & Rausch Chocolate Shop
㉗ B-Flat Acoustic Music & Jazz Club

ple. It's dressy, with fun sidewalk seating or a dark and elegant interior (€9-18 starters, €16-24 main dishes, daily 11:00-24:00, Charlottenstrasse 56, tel. 030/202-9540).

Augustiner am Gendarmenmarkt, next door to Lutter & Wegner, lines its sidewalk with trademark Bavarian white-and-blue-checkerboard tablecloths; inside, you'll find a classic Bavarian beer-hall atmosphere. Less pretentious than its neighbor, it offers good beer and affordable Bavarian classics in an equally appealing location (€6-12 light meals, €10-20 bigger meals, daily 10:00-24:00, Charlottenstrasse 55, tel. 030/2045-4020).

Galeries Lafayette Food Circus is a French festival of fun eateries in the basement of the landmark department store. You'll find a good deli and prepared-food stands, dishing up cuisine that's good-quality but not cheap (most options €10-15, cheaper €5-10 sandwiches and savory crêpes, Mon-Sat 10:00-20:00, closed Sun, Friedrichstrasse 76-78, U-Bahn: Französische Strasse, tel. 030/209-480).

Between the River and Prenzlauer Berg

All of these eateries are within a 10-minute walk of the Hackescher Markt S-Bahn station.

Near Hackescher Markt

Hasir Turkish Restaurant is your chance to dine with candles, hardwood floors, and happy Berliners savoring meaty Anatolian specialties. As Berlin is the world's largest Turkish city outside of Asia Minor, it's no wonder you can find truly good Turkish restaurants here. This restaurant, in a courtyard next to the Hackesche Höfe shopping complex, offers indoor and outdoor tables filled with an enthusiastic local crowd. The service can be questionable, so bring some patience (€7 starters, €15-20 main dishes, large and splittable portions, daily 12:00-24:00, in late evening the courtyard is dominated by an unpleasantly loud underground disco, a block from the Hackescher Markt S-Bahn station at Oranienburger Strasse 4, tel. 030/2804-1616).

Weihenstephaner Bavarian Restaurant serves upmarket traditional Bavarian food for around €10-15 a plate; offers an atmospheric cellar, an inner courtyard, and a busy people-watching streetside terrace; and, of course, has excellent beer (daily 11:00-23:00, Neue Promenade 5 at Hackescher Markt, tel. 030/8471-0760).

On or near Oranienburger Strasse

Oranienburger Strasse, a few blocks west of Hackescher Markt, is busy with happy eaters. Restaurants on this stretch come with happy hours and lots of cocktails. **Aufsturz,** a lively pub, has a huge selection of beer and whisky and dishes up "traditional

Berliner pub grub" to a young crowd (Oranienburger Strasse 67). **Amrit Lounge** is great on a warm evening if you'd like Indian food outdoors with an umbrellas-in-your-drink Caribbean ambience (€6 cocktails, €10-14 meals, long hours daily, Oranienburger Strasse 45). Next door is **QBA,** a fun Cuban bar and restaurant.

BERLIN

Schwarzwaldstuben, between Oranienburger Strasse and Rosenthaler Platz, is a Black Forest-themed pub—which explains the antlers, cuckoo clocks, and painting of a thick forest on the wall. It's friendly, with good service, food, and prices. The staff chooses the music (often rock or jazz), and the ambience is warm and welcoming. If they're full, you can eat at the long bar or at one of the sidewalk tables (€7-16 meals, daily 9:00-23:00, Tucholskystrasse 48, tel. 030/2809-8084).

Gipsy Restaurant serves good, reasonably priced German and Italian dishes, including brats, pizza, and homemade cakes, in a bohemian-chic atmosphere—especially nice on a balmy evening outdoors (daily 12:30-23:00, at Clärchens Ballhaus, Auguststrasse 24, tel. 030/282-9295).

Near Rosenthaler Platz

Surrounding the U8: Rosenthaler Platz station, a short stroll or tram ride from the Hackescher Markt S-Bahn station, and an easy walk from the Oranienburger Strasse action, this busy neighborhood has a few enticing options.

My Smart Break is a great spot to pick up a freshly made deli sandwich, hummus plate, salad, fresh-squeezed juice, or other quick, tasty, healthy snack. Linger in the interior, grab one of the few sidewalk tables, or take your food to munch on the go (€5-8 sandwiches, daily 8:00-23:00, Rosenthaler Strasse 67, tel. 030/2390-0303).

Transit is a stylish, innovative, affordable Thai/Indonesian/pan-Asian small-plates restaurant. Sit at one of the long shared tables and dig into a creative menu of €3 small plates and €8 big plates. Two people can make a filling meal out of three or four dishes (daily 11:00-24:00, cash only, Rosenthaler Strasse 68, tel. 030/2478-1645).

Restaurant Simon dishes up tasty Italian and German specialties—enjoy them either in the restaurant's simple yet atmospheric interior, or opt for streetside seating right on the park across the street (€8-15 main dishes, Mon-Sat 17:00-23:00, closed Sun, cash only, Auguststrasse 53, at intersection with Kleine Auguststrasse, tel. 030/2789-0300).

In Prenzlauer Berg

Prenzlauer Berg is packed with fine restaurants—German, ethnic, and everything in between. Even if you're not staying in this area, it's worth venturing here for dinner. Before making a choice, I'd spend at least a half-hour strolling and browsing through this bohemian wonderland of creative eateries.

Near Eberswalder Strasse

The area surrounding the elevated Eberswalder Strasse U-Bahn station is the epicenter of Prenzlauer Berg—a young, hip, and edgy place to eat and drink. While a bit farther north than other areas I recommend (and a 10- to 15-minute walk from most of my recommended hotels), it's worth the trip to immerse yourself in quintessential Prenzlauer Berg.

Prater Biergarten offers two great eating opportunities: a rustic indoor restaurant and a mellow, shaded, super-cheap, and family-friendly outdoor beer garden (with a playground)—each proudly pouring Prater's own microbrew. In the beer garden—Berlin's oldest—you step up to the counter and order (simple €3-6 plates and an intriguing selection of beer munchies, daily in good weather 12:00-24:00). The restaurant serves serious traditional *Biergarten* cuisine and good salads (€10-20 plates, Mon-Sat 18:00-24:00, Sun from 12:00, cash only, Kastanienallee 7, tel. 030/448-5688).

Zum Schusterjungen Speisegaststätte ("The Cobbler's Apprentice") is a classic old-school, German-with-attitude eatery that retains its circa-1986 DDR decor. Famous for its filling €9-13 meals (including various types of schnitzel and Berlin classics such as pork knuckle), it's a no-frills place with quality ingredients and a strong local following. It serves the needs of those Berliners lamenting the disappearance of solid, traditional German cooking amid the flood of ethnic eateries (small 40-seat dining hall plus outdoor tables, daily 12:00-24:00, corner of Lychener Strasse and Danziger Strasse 9, tel. 030/442-7654).

La Bodeguita del Medio Cuban Bar Restaurant is purely fun-loving Cuba—graffiti-caked walls, Che Guevara posters, animated staff, and an ambience that makes you want to dance. Come early to eat or late to drink. This restaurant has been here since 1994—and in fast-changing Prenzlauer Berg, that's an eternity. The German-Cuban couple who run it take pride in their food, and the main dishes are big enough to split. You can even puff a Cuban cigar at the sidewalk tables (€4-10 tapas, €9 Cuban ribs and salad, Tue-Sun 18:00-24:00, closed Mon, cash only, a block from U2: Eberswalder Strasse at Lychener Strasse 6, tel. 030/4050-0601).

Konnopke's Imbiss, a super-cheap German-style sausage stand, has been a Berlin institution for more than 70 years—it was family-owned even during DDR times. Berliners say Konnopke's cooks up some of the city's best *Currywurst* (€2.20). Located beneath the U2 viaduct, the stand was demolished in 2010 during

BERLIN

roadwork. Berliners rioted, and Konnopke's was rebuilt in a slick glass-and-steel hut (Mon-Fri 9:00-20:00, Sat from 11:30, closed Sun; Kastanienallee dead-ends at the elevated train tracks, and under them you'll find Konnopke's at Schönhauser Allee 44A, tel. 030/442-7765). Don't confuse this with the nearby Currystation—look for the real Konnopke's.

Restaurant Die Schule is a modern place with a no-frills style where you can sample traditional German dishes tapas-style. Assemble a collection of little €2.50 plates of old-fashioned German food you might not try otherwise (€8-18 main dishes, €29 three-course meal, good indoor and outdoor seating, daily 11:00-22:00, Kastanienallee 82, tel. 030/780-089-550).

After-Dinner Dessert and Drinks: Oodles of characteristic funky pubs and nightspots fill the area around Helmholtzplatz (and elsewhere in Prenzlauer Berg). Oderberger Strasse is a fun zone to explore. Along here, **Kauf Dich Glücklich** makes a great capper to a Prenzlauer Berg dinner. It serves an enticing array of sweet Belgian waffles and ice cream in a candy-sprinkled, bohemian lounge on a great Prenzlauer Berg street (Mon-Fri 11:00-24:00, Sat-Sun from 10:00, indoor and outdoor seating—or get your dessert to go, wait possible on busy nights, Oderberger Strasse 44, tel. 030/4862-3292).

Near Kollwitzplatz

This square, home of the DDR student resistance in 1980s, is now trendy and upscale, popular with hip parents who take their hip kids to the leafy playground park at its center. It's an especially good area to prowl among upmarket restaurants—walk the square and choose. Just about every option offers sidewalk seats in the summer (great on a balmy evening). It's a long block up Kollwitzstrasse from U2: Senefelderplatz.

Gugelhof, right on Kollwitzplatz, is an institution famous for its Alsatian German cuisine. You'll enjoy French quality with German proportions. It's highly regarded, with a boisterous and enthusiastic local crowd filling its minimalist yet classy interior. In good weather, outdoor seating sprawls along its sidewalk. Their fixed-price meals are fun, and they welcome swapping (€25-35 three-course meals, €6-11 starters, €10-16 main dishes, Mon-Fri 17:00-23:00, Sat-Sun from 10:00, reservations smart, where Knaackstrasse meets Kollwitzplatz, tel. 030/442-9229, www.gugelhof.de).

Metzer Eck is a time-warp *Kneipe* with cozy charm and a family tradition dating to 1913. It serves cheap, basic, typical Berlin food with five beers on tap, including the Czech Budvar (€5-10 meals, Mon-Fri 16:00-24:00, Sat from 18:00, closed Sun, Metzer Strasse 33, on the corner with Strassburger Strasse, tel. 030/442-7656).

IN WESTERN BERLIN
Near Savignyplatz

Many good restaurants are on or within 100 yards of Savignyplatz, near my recommended western Berlin hotels. Savignyplatz is lined with attractive, relaxed, mostly Mediterranean-style places. Take a walk and survey these; continue your stroll along Bleibtreustrasse to discover many trendier, more creative little eateries.

Restaurant Marjellchen is a trip to East Prussia. Dine in a soft, jazzy elegance in one of two six-table rooms. While it doesn't have to be expensive (€12-20 main courses), plan to go the whole nine yards here, as this can be a great experience, with caring service. The menu is inviting, and the place family-run—all the recipes were brought to Berlin by the owner's East Prussian mother after World War II. Reservations are smart (daily 17:00-22:30, Mommsenstrasse 9, tel. 030/883-2676, www.marjellchen-berlin.de).

Restaurant Leibniz-Klause is a good place for a dressy German meal. You'll enjoy upscale presentation on white tablecloths, hunter-sized portions, service that's both friendly and professional, and no pretense. Their *Berliner Riesen-Eisbein* ("super pork-leg on the bone"), with sauerkraut and horseradish, will stir even the tiniest amount of Teutonic blood in your veins (€11-22 plates, good indoor and outdoor seating, daily 12:00-23:30, Leibnizstrasse near corner with Mommsenstrasse, tel. 030/323-7068).

Dicke Wirtin ("Fat Innkeeper") is a pub with traditional old-Berlin *Kneipe* atmosphere, six good beers on tap, and solid home cooking at reasonable prices—such as their famously cheap *Gulaschsuppe* (€4.60). Their interior is fun and pubby, with soccer on the TV; their streetside tables are also inviting. Pickled eggs are on the bar—ask about how these can help you avoid a hangover (€6-16 main dishes, Bavarian Andechs beer on tap, daily 11:00-23:00, dinner served from 18:00, just off Savignyplatz at Carmerstrasse 9, tel. 030/312-4952).

Weyers offers modern German cuisine in a simple, elegant setting, with dining tables in the summer spilling out into the idyllic neighborhood park in front (€10-16 dishes, daily 8:00-24:00, facing Ludwigkirchplatz at corner of Pariser Strasse and Pfalzburger Strasse, tel. 030/881-9378).

Café Literaturhaus is a neighborhood favorite for a light meal, sandwich, or dessert (but also serves an elegant if limited menu of full meals). It has the ambience of an Old World villa with a big garden perfect for their evening poetry readings (€7 small tea sandwiches, €14-27 meals, daily 9:30-23:00, smart to reserve for dinner if eating inside, Fasanenstrasse 23, tel. 030/882-5414).

Die Zwölf Apostel ("The Twelve Apostles") is popular for good Italian food. Choose between indoors with candlelit ambience, outdoors on a sun-dappled patio, or overlooking the people parade on an atmospherically narrow pedestrian street. A local crowd packs this restaurant for €12 pizzas and €15-20 meals (long hours daily, cash only, immediately across from Savignyplatz S-Bahn entrance, Bleibtreustrasse 49, tel. 030/312-1433).

Zillemarkt Restaurant, which feels like an old-time Berlin *Biergarten,* serves traditional Berlin specialties in the garden or in the rustic candlelit interior. Their *Berliner Allerlei* is a fun way to sample a bit of cabbage, pork, sausage, potatoes, and more (for a minimum of two people...but it can feed up to five). They have their own microbrew (€10-15 meals, daily 12:00-24:00, near the S-Bahn tracks at Bleibtreustrasse 48A, tel. 030/881-7040).

Supermarket: The neighborhood grocery store is **Ullrich** (Mon-Sat 9:00-22:00, Sun from 11:00, Kantstrasse 7, under the tracks near Bahnhof Zoo). There's plenty of fast food near Bahnhof Zoo and on Ku'damm.

Near Bahnhof Zoo

Schleusenkrug beer garden is hidden in the park overlooking a canal between the Bahnhof Zoo and Tiergarten stations. Choose from an ever-changing self-service menu of huge salads, pasta, and some German dishes (€8-15 plates, daily 10:00-24:00, food served 12:00-22:00, cash only; from Bahnhof Zoo, it's a 5-minute walk, following the path into the park between the zoo and train tracks; tel. 030/313-9909).

Self-Service Cafeterias: The top floor of the famous department store, **KaDeWe,** holds the Winter Garden Buffet view cafeteria, and its sixth-floor deli/food department is a picnicker's nirvana. Its arterials are clogged with more than 1,000 kinds of sausage and 1,500 types of cheese (daily 10:00-20:00, Fri until 21:00, Sat from 9:30, closed Sun, U-Bahn: Wittenbergplatz).

Berlin Connections

BY TRAIN

Berlin's Hauptbahnhof has emerged as the city's single, massive central station, with its other train stations now wilted into glorified subway stations. Virtually all long-distance trains pass through the Hauptbahnhof. Before buying a ticket for any long train ride from Berlin (over 7 hours), consider taking a cheap flight instead (buy it well in advance to get a super fare). Train info: Toll tel. 0180-699-6633, www.bahn.com.

EurAide, an agent of Deutsche Bahn, sells reservations for high-speed and overnight trains, with staff that can answer your travel questions in English (located in the *Hauptbahnhof*).

From Berlin by Train to: Potsdam (2/hour, 30 minutes on RE1 train; or take S-Bahn from other points in Berlin, S-1 direct, S-7 with a change at Wannsee, 6/hour, 30-50 minutes), **Oranienburg** and Sachsenhausen Concentration Camp Memorial (hourly, 25 minutes; or take the S-1 line from Friedrichstrasse or other stops in town, 3/hour, 50 minutes), **Wittenberg** (a.k.a. *Lutherstadt Wittenberg,* hourly on ICE, 45 minutes; also every 2 hours on slower regional train, 1.5 hours), **Dresden** (every 2 hours, more with a transfer in Leipzig, 2.5 hours), **Leipzig** (hourly direct, 1.5 hours), **Erfurt** (hourly, 2.5-3 hours, transfer in Leipzig or Naumburg/Saale), **Eisenach** and Wartburg Castle (hourly, 3-3.5 hours, transfer in Leipzig or Naumburg/Saale), **Hamburg** (1-2/hour direct, 2 hours), **Frankfurt** (hourly, 4 hours), **Bacharach** (hourly, 7 hours, 1-3 changes), **Würzburg** (hourly, 4 hours, change in Göttingen or Fulda), **Rothenburg** (hourly, 5.5 hours, 3 changes), **Nürnberg** (hourly, 4.5 hours), **Munich** (1-2/hour, 6.5 hours, every 2 hours direct, otherwise change in Göttingen, night train possible), **Cologne** (hourly, 4.5 hours, night train possible), **Amsterdam** (roughly hourly to Amsterdam Zuid, 6.5 hours; wise to reserve in advance), **Budapest** (3/day including one overnight, 12-14 hours, these go via Czech Republic and Slovakia; if your rail pass doesn't cover these countries, save money on a longer route via Vienna), **Copenhagen** (8/day, 8 hours, reservation required, change in Hamburg, 1/day direct departs at 11:25; also consider direct overnight train-plus-ferry route to Malmö Central Station, Sweden—just 20 minutes from Copenhagen and covered by a rail pass that includes Germany or Sweden), **London** (8/day, 11-13 hours, 2-3 changes—you're better off flying cheap, even if you have a rail pass), **Paris** (11/day, 10 hours, change in Cologne—via Belgium—or in Mannheim), **Zürich** (1-2 hour, 9 hours, transfer in Basel; 1 direct 11-hour night train), **Prague** (6/day direct, 5.5 hours, wise to reserve in advance), **Warsaw** (6/day, 6.5 hours, reservations required on all Warsaw-bound trains), **Kraków** (1/day direct, 10 hours; 2 more with transfer in Warsaw, 8.5 hours), **Vienna** (9/day, most with 1-2 changes, 1/day plus 1/night are direct, 11 hours; some via Czech Republic, but trains with a change in Nürnberg, Munich, or Würzburg avoid that country—useful if it's not covered by your rail pass).

Night trains run from Berlin to these cities: Munich, Cologne, Vienna, Budapest, Basel, and Zürich. A *Liegeplatz,* a.k.a. *couchette* berth (€15-36), is a great deal; inquire at EurAide at the

Hauptbahnhof for details. Beds generally cost the same whether you have a first- or second-class ticket or rail pass. Trains are often full, so reserve your *couchette* a few days in advance from any travel agency or major train station in Europe.

BY BUS

The city's bus station, **ZOB** (Zentraler Omnibusbahnhof), is west of Bahnhof Zoo, in Charlottenburg (Masurenallee 4-6, U2: Kaiserdamm). **MeinFernBus, Flix, Berlin Linien**, and **Eurolines** all operate from here to locations around Germany and Europe.

BY PLANE

Berlin is the continental European hub for budget airlines such as easyJet (lots of flights to Spain, Italy, Eastern Europe, the Baltics, and more—book long in advance to get best fares, www.easyjet.com). Ryanair (www.ryanair.com), Air Berlin (www.airberlin.com), and German Wings (www.germanwings.com) make the London-Berlin trip (and other routes) dirt-cheap, so consider this option before booking an overnight train. Consequently, British visitors to the city are now outnumbered only by Americans.

Berlin is trying to finish construction of its new airport, **Willy Brandt Berlin-Brandenburg International**, located about 13 miles from central Berlin (airport code: BER), but the project has been perennially delayed. You'll most likely use **Tegel Airport,** which is four miles from the center (airport code: TXL). Bus #TXL goes between the airport, the Hauptbahnhof (stops by Washingtonplatz entrance), and Alexanderplatz in eastern Berlin. For western Berlin, take bus #X9 to Bahnhof Zoo, or slower bus #109 to Ku'damm and Bahnhof Zoo (€2.70). Bus #128 goes to northern Berlin. A taxi from Tegel Airport costs about €30 to Alexanderplatz or €20 to Bahnhof Zoo (taxis from Tegel levy a €0.50 surcharge).

Most flights from the east and discount airlines arrive at **Schönefeld Airport** (12.5 miles from center). From the old Schönefeld arrivals hall, it's a three-minute walk to the train station, where you can catch a regional express train into the city (ignore the S-Bahn, as there are no direct S-Bahn trains to the city center). Airport Express RE and RB trains go directly to Ostbahnhof, Alexanderplatz, Friedrichstrasse, Hauptbahnhof, and Bahnhof Zoo (€3.30, 2/hour, direction: Nauen or Dessau, rail pass valid). A taxi to the city center costs about €35.

BY CRUISE SHIP FROM THE PORT OF WARNEMÜNDE

Many cruise lines advertise a stop in "Berlin," but the ships actually put in at the Baltic seaside town of Warnemünde—a whopping 150 miles north of downtown Berlin. By train, by tour bus, or by Porsche on the autobahn, plan on at least six hours of travel time round-trip between Warnemünde and Berlin. The easiest option is to book a package excursion from your cruise line. You can also book a tour directly with a local Berlin-based operator such as Original Berlin Walks). Otherwise, several train connections run each day from Warnemünde's train station to Berlin (roughly every 2 hours, 3 hours, transfer in Rostock).

For much more detail on how to get into Berlin and spend your time once there, pick up the *Rick Steves Northern European Cruise Ports* guidebook.

NEAR BERLIN

Potsdam • Sachsenhausen Concentration Camp Memorial

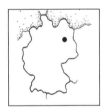

While you could spend days in Berlin and not run out of things to do, a few worthwhile side-trips are just outside the city center (within an hour of downtown Berlin). Frederick the Great's opulent palace playground at Potsdam is a hit with those who enjoy ornate interiors and pretty parks. On the opposite side of Berlin—and the sightseeing spectrum—Sachsenhausen Concentration Camp Memorial provides a somber look at the Nazis' mass production of death during the Holocaust. (A third side-trip possibility—the small town of Wittenberg, with excellent Martin Luther-related sights—is within a 45-minute train ride of Berlin.) Dresden and Leipzig also work as day trips from Berlin.

PLANNING YOUR TIME

Potsdam or Sachsenhausen can take anywhere from a half-day to a full day of your time, depending on your interests. Think twice before visiting Potsdam on a Monday (when Sanssouci Palace is closed) or a Tuesday (when the New Palace is closed); make your pilgrimage to Sachsenhausen any day but Monday (when the grounds are open but interior exhibits are closed).

Potsdam: It takes about an hour one-way from downtown Berlin to reach the palaces at Potsdam (including the train to Potsdam, then a bus or bike ride to the palaces). The two main palaces—Sanssouci and the New Palace—are quite different but complementary, and connected by a huge park. Visiting either takes about an hour to an hour and a half, plus a potential wait for your Sanssouci entry time (arrive at Sanssouci by 10:00 to avoid waiting in the ticket line). Give yourself five hours round-trip to do the whole shebang. On a quicker visit, you can make a beeline from the

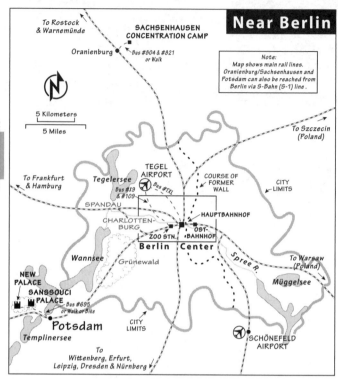

NEAR BERLIN

To Rostock & Warnemünde

SACHSENHAUSEN CONCENTRATION CAMP

Near Berlin

Oranienburg ● ⟵Bus #804 & #821 or Walk

Note:
Map shows main rail lines.
Oranienburg/Sachsenhausen and
Potsdam can also be reached from
Berlin via S-Bahn (S-1) line.

5 Kilometers

5 Miles

To Szczecin (Poland)

TEGEL AIRPORT

COURSE OF FORMER WALL

CITY LIMITS

To Frankfurt & Hamburg

Tegelersee

Bus #X9 & #109

Bus #TXL

SPANDAU

HAUPTBAHNHOF

CHARLOTTEN-BURG

ZOO STN.

OST-BAHNHOF

Berlin Center

Wannsee

Grünewald

Spree R.

To Warsaw (Poland)

Müggelsee

NEW PALACE

SANSSOUCI PALACE

Bus #695 or Walk or Bike

Potsdam

Templinersee

CITY LIMITS

SCHÖNEFELD AIRPORT

To Wittenberg, Erfurt, Leipzig, Dresden & Nürnberg

train station to your choice of palaces (Sanssouci is closer and more intimate, but may require a wait; New Palace is grander but at the far end of the park). It's tempting to stretch your Potsdam visit into a full day so you can linger in the park and tour other royal buildings, poke around the inviting town center of Potsdam, or visit nearby attractions (such as Cecilienhof, the site of the post-WWII Potsdam Conference attended by Churchill, Stalin, and Truman).

Avid cyclists can rent a bike and combine a visit to Potsdam with an enjoyable ride along skinny lakes and through green parklands back into the city.

Sachsenhausen: Two hours at the camp is just enough for a quick walk through the grounds; three hours is a minimum if you want to read the many worthwhile exhibits. Factoring in transit time, leave yourself at least six hours round-trip from central Berlin.

Both: For an exhausting day of contrasts, you could get an early start to visit Sachsenhausen (opens at 8:30), munch a picnic lunch on the train down to Potsdam (connected by the S-1 line in about 1.5 hours; also several basic lunch options in Potsdam train station), and tour Frederick the Great's palaces before collapsing on an evening train back to Berlin.

Potsdam

Featuring a lush park strewn with the escapist whimsies of Frederick the Great, the sleepy town of Potsdam has long been Ber-

lin's holiday retreat. It's your best opportunity to get a taste of Prussia's Hohenzollern royalty. While Potsdam's palaces are impressive, they don't quite crack Europe's top 10—perhaps because the audioguides don't inject the Hohenzollerns' personalities into the place (or maybe the Hohenzollerns really were that boring). But Potsdam is convenient to reach from downtown Berlin, and it makes for a great break from the city's heavy history. It's also ideal on a sunny day, thanks to its strolling- and picnic-friendly park.

GETTING TO POTSDAM

Potsdam is about 15 miles southwest of Berlin. You have two easy train options for zipping from the city to Potsdam's Hauptbahnhof (main train station; round-trip covered by €7.40 Berlin transit day pass with zones ABC). Direct **Regional Express/RE1 trains** depart twice hourly from Berlin's Bahnhof Zoo (20 minutes to Potsdam), Hauptbahnhof (30 minutes), and Friedrichstrasse (35 minutes; any train to Brandenburg or Magdeburg stops in Potsdam). Note: Some RE1 trains continue past the Potsdam Hauptbahnhof to a stop called Park Sanssouci, which is even closer to the palaces (check the schedule).

The **S-Bahn** is slightly slower, but more frequent and handier from some areas of Berlin. The S-1 line goes directly to Potsdam from Potsdamer Platz, Brandenburger Tor, Friedrichstrasse, and Oranienburger Strasse (6/hour, 30-45 minutes depending on starting point). The S-7 line, which requires a transfer at Wannsee, leaves from Alexanderplatz, Hackescher Markt, Friedrichstrasse, Berlin Hauptbahnhof, Bahnhof Zoo, Savignyplatz, and other city-center stations; after the line ends at Wannsee, cross the platform to an S-1 train, and ride it three more stops to Potsdam (6/hour, about 50 minutes total from downtown Berlin).

Orientation to Potsdam

The city center is enjoyable to explore, but most visitors head right to Frederick the Great's palaces, which surround the sprawling Sanssouci Park at the northwest edge of town.

TOURIST INFORMATION

A handy TI is inside Potsdam's **train station** (Mon-Sat 9:30-20:00, Sun 10:00-16:00, tel. 0331/2755-8899, www.potsdamtourismus. de). Another TI branch, closer to the **town center** at Luisenplatz, is less convenient for most visitors (Mon-Sat 9:30-18:00, Sun 9:30-16:00, shorter hours Nov-March, Brandenburger Strasse 3, same contact info as main branch). Get a map and ask about bus tours if you're interested (see "Tours in Potsdam," later).

The **palace information office** is very helpful, with friendly English-speaking staff. It's across the street from the windmill near the Sanssouci entrance (daily April-Oct 8:30-18:00, Nov-March 8:30-17:00, tel. 0331/969-4200—then press 1, www.spsg. de; clean WC in same building).

To supplement the English tour handouts and audioguides at the palaces, consider picking up the blue "official guide" booklets (available individually for each of the sights, €4 apiece at palace info office and gift shops).

ARRIVAL IN POTSDAM

From Potsdam's **main train station** you have several options for reaching the palaces. It's a long (but scenic) 45-minute walk (get directions and pick up a map at the TI; exit the station on the opposite side from the bus/tram stops), a 20-minute bike ride (bike rental under track 6/7—see "By Bike," next), or a 10- to 15-minute transit ride. To find the bus/tram stops, exit the station following *ReiseZentrum* signs; this takes you out the main door, where you'll find a row of stops.

If you arrive at Potsdam's **Park Sanssouci Station,** just walk straight out and head up the boulevard called Am Neuen Palais, with the big park on your right. In about 10 minutes, you'll reach the New Palace.

GETTING AROUND POTSDAM

By Bike: Flat Potsdam is ideal by bike, with one caveat: Within Sanssouci Park you're restricted to a bike path between the palaces; you can't even walk with a bike anywhere else in the park. At the main train station, **Pedales** rents bikes and provides a map showing recommended routes (€11, €9 after 14:00, helmet-€2, daily 9:30-19:00, passport required—other ID won't work, under escalator along platform 6/7, tel. 0331/7480-057). From the station it's a pleasant and well-signed 20-minute ride to Sanssouci Palace.

By Bus or Tram: Various **buses** leave the station about every 10 minutes (single ride-€1.90, all-day pass-€4, buy tickets from machine on bus, also covered by any Berlin pass with zones ABC). Convenient but packed bus #695 cruises through Potsdam's appealing town center, stopping first at Sanssouci, then at the New Palace (3/hour, 15-20 minutes, leaves from lane 4). Buses #606 and #605 stop only at the New Palace (3/hour apiece, 10-15 minutes, both leave from lane 4). If you're up for a scenic walk up the terraced palace gardens, another option is to take **tram** #91 to Luisenplatz (3/hour, 8 minutes, leaves from lane 1), then walk 20 minutes through the park, which lets you enjoy a classic view of Sanssouci Palace.

Tours in Potsdam

Local Tours
Various bus tours (including hop-on, hop-off options) conveniently connect this town's spread-out sights. Pick up brochures at the TI or check their website (www.potsdamtourismus.de).

Tours from Berlin
Original Berlin Walks and Brewer's Berlin Tours offer inexpensive all-day tours from Berlin to Potsdam (about €15, small groups, English-language only, reservations not necessary, admissions and public transportation not included, doesn't actually go into Sanssouci Palace). **Original Berlin Walks'** tour leaves Berlin at 9:40 every Thursday and Sunday from April through October. The guide takes you to Cecilienhof Palace, through pleasant green landscapes to the historic heart of Potsdam for lunch, and finishes outside Sanssouci Palace. **Brewer's Berlin Tours** depart Berlin at 10:20 on Wednesdays and Saturdays from May through October.

Sights in Potsdam

FREDERICK THE GREAT'S PALACES

Frederick the Great was a dynamic 18th-century ruler who put Prussia on the map with his merciless military prowess. Yet he also had tender affection for the finer things in

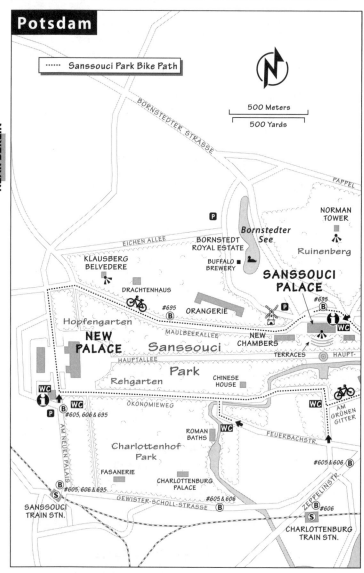

Potsdam

..... Sanssouci Park Bike Path

500 Meters
500 Yards

NEAR BERLIN

BORNSTEDTER STRASSE

PAPPEL

NORMAN TOWER

Bornstedter See

Ruinenberg

EICHEN ALLEE

BORNSTEDT ROYAL ESTATE

BUFFALO BREWERY

SANSSOUCI PALACE

KLAUSBERG BELVEDERE

DRACHTENHAUS

#695

ORANGERIE

#695

Hopfengarten

MAULBEERALLEE

NEW CHAMBERS

NEW PALACE

Sanssouci

HAUPTALLEE

TERRACES

HAUPT-

Park

Rehgarten

CHINESE HOUSE

WC

WC

ÖKONOMIEWEG

AM GRÜNEN GITTER

#605, 606 & 695

ROMAN BATHS

WC

FEUERBACHSTR.

AM NEUEN PALAIS

Charlottenhof Park

FASANERIE

CHARLOTTENBURG PALACE

#605 & 606

#605, 606 & 695

GEWISTER-SCHOLL-STRASSE

#605 & 606

ZEPPELINSTR.

#606

SANSSOUCI TRAIN STN.

CHARLOTTENBURG TRAIN STN.

life: art, architecture, gardens, literature, and other distinguished pursuits. During his reign, Frederick built an impressive ensemble of palaces and other grand buildings around Sanssouci Park, with the two top palaces located at either end. Frederick's super-Rococo Sanssouci Palace is dazzling, while his equally extravagant New Palace was built to wow guests and disprove rumors that Prussia was running out of money after the costly Seven Years' War.

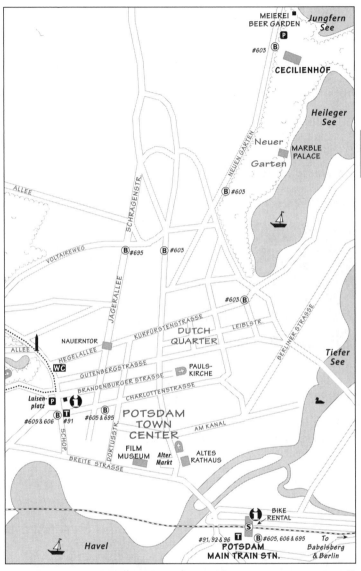

Getting Between the Palaces: It's about a 30-minute walk between Sanssouci and the New Palace, and about 10 minutes by bike. Otherwise you can hop on bus #695, which takes you between the palaces in either direction (covered by a cheap €1.40 *Kurzstrecke* ticket, as well as by a Berlin transit pass with zones ABC). If you do walk, you'll find the park wilder, more forested, and less carefully manicured than those in other big-league European palace complexes (such as Versailles or Vienna's Schönbrunn). The park's €2 suggested donation comes with a helpful map.

Combo-Ticket: The €19 combo-ticket, covering nearly all the royal buildings in the park, is worthwhile only if you're visiting Sanssouci, the New Palace, and at least one other sight (though for most visitors, those two are enough). It's sold only at the Sanssouci Palace ticket office and the New Palace visitors center.

Information: Tel. 0331/969-4200, www.spsg.de.

Photos: You'll pay a €3 fee for a one-day pass to take photos (without flash) at all royal buildings.

▲▲Sanssouci Palace

Sans souci means "without a care," and this was the carefree summer home of Frederick the Great (built 1745-1747). Of all the palatial

buildings scattered around Potsdam, this was his actual residence. While the palace is small and the audioguide does little to capture the personality of its former resident, it's worth seeing for its opulence.

Cost and Hours: €12, €8 Nov-March, includes audioguide; April-Oct Tue-Sun 10:00-18:00, Nov-March Tue-Sun 10:00-17:00, closed Mon year-round; in winter, entrance is with a live guided German tour only (departs about every 20 minutes)—about once an hour, they let English speakers with audioguides tag along.

Crowd-Beating Tips: At this popular sight, your ticket comes with an appointed entry time. (Tickets are sold for the same day only.) For the most stress-free visit, come early: In the summer, if you arrive by 10:00 (when the ticket office opens), you'll get right in. If you arrive after 11:00, plan to stand in line to buy your ticket. You'll probably have to wait for your entry time, too—usually an hour or two later. Pass this time visiting the Ladies' Wing (open only on weekends in summer) and the Palace Kitchen or by exploring the sprawling gardens. If you have a very long wait, zip over to visit the New Palace, then circle back to Sanssouci.

Visiting the Palace: Your ticket covers three parts—The Ladies' Wing (to the left as you face the palace from the front/garden side); the Palace Kitchen (to the right); and the living quarters and festival halls (the main, central part). You can visit the first two sights anytime, but you must report to the main part of the palace at the time noted on your ticket (you'll receive your audioguide there).

The **Ladies' Wing (Damenflügel),** worth a visit only if you have time to kill (and maybe not even then), contains apartments for ladies-in-waiting and servants. Borrow the dull English descriptions and walk past rooms cluttered with cutesy decor. The servants' quarters upstairs have been turned into a painting gallery.

At the **Palace Kitchen (Schlossküche),** see well-preserved mid-19th-century cooking equipment (with posted English information). Hike down the tight spiral staircase to the wine cellar, which features an exhibit about the grapes that were grown on the terraced vineyards out front.

The **Main Palace** was where Frederick the Great spent his summers. The dry audioguide narrates your stroll through the classic Rococo interior, where golden grapevines climb the walls and frame the windows. First explore the Royal Apartments, containing one of Frederick's three libraries (he found it easier to buy extra copies of books rather than move them around), the "study bedroom" where he lived and worked, and the chair where he died. The domed, central Marble Hall resembles the Pantheon in Rome (on a smaller scale), with an oblong oculus, inlaid marble floors, and Corinthian columns made of Carrara marble.

Finally you'll visit the guest rooms, most of which exit straight out onto the delightful terrace. Each room is decorated differently: Chinese, Italian, and so on; the niche at the back was for a bed. The happiest is the yellow Voltaire Room, where realistic animals and flowers dangle from the walls and ceiling. As you exit (through the servants' quarters), keep an eye out for the giant portrait of Frederick by Andy Warhol.

▲▲New Palace (Neues Palais)

This gigantic showpiece palace (with more than 200 rooms) is, in some ways, more impressive than the intimate Sanssouci. While

Frederick the Great lived primarily at Sanssouci, he built the New Palace later (1763-1769) to host guests and dazzle visiting dignitaries. And unlike at Sanssouci, there's rarely a long wait to buy tickets or enter the palace. The palace is undergoing renovation in 2016, so you'll likely encounter scaffolding and a few rooms (such as the famed Marble Hall) will be off-limits.

Cost and Hours: €8, includes audioguide, April-Oct Wed-Mon 10:00-18:00, Nov-March Wed-Mon 10:00-17:00, closed Tue year-round. Tickets are available only at the shop across the way, not in the palace itself. To see the king's ho-hum apartments—eight small rooms that are a watered-down version of what you'll see at Sanssouci—you must take a 45-minute tour in German (May-Oct daily at 10:00, 11:00, 14:00, and 16:00). During the off-season (Nov-March), the king's apartments are closed, and you can visit the rest of the New Palace by tagging along with a German tour (with an English audioguide; may have to wait up to 30 minutes for next tour). Currently the palace has no WC for visitors—the closest one is in the shop/ticket office.

NEAR BERLIN

Visiting the Palace: The tour includes an overly detailed, one-hour English audioguide that takes you through the ornate halls (you can always skip ahead if you feel fatigued). Downstairs has the eight suites of the Lower Princes' Apartments, which accommodated guests and royal family members. In the 19th and early 20th century, German emperors Frederick III (different from the earlier Frederick who built the place) and Wilhelm II (the last Kaiser) resided here. The Gentlemen's Bedchamber holds the red-canopy bed where Kaiser Frederick III died in 1888. The Ladies' Bedchamber is a reminder that noblemen and their wives slept separately.

Upstairs, the Upper Princes' Quarters include a small blue-tiled bathroom that was later installed for Kaiser Wilhelm II. You'll also find Wilhelm's bedroom, as well as a small painting gallery with portraits of Frederick the Great and Russia's Catherine the Great (who was actually a German princess). For one wing you'll need to don a pair of loaner slippers to protect the floors. Through the windows, enjoy the views of the gardens, which recede into the horizon.

Other Palaces

The two main palaces (Sanssouci and the New Palace) are just the beginning. The sprawling Sanssouci Park contains a variety of other

palaces and royal buildings, many of which you can enter. Popular options include the Italian-style **Orangerie** (the last and largest palace in the park, closed for renovation until 2018); the **New Chambers** (a royal guest house); the **Chinese House;** and other viewpoints, including the **Klausberg Belvedere** and the **Norman Tower.**

Cost and Hours: Each has its own entry fee (€2-4; all but Belvedere covered by €19 combo-ticket) and hours, some are open weekends only (get a complete list from Potsdam TI or palace information office).

Bornstedt Royal Estate (Krongut Bornstedt)

Designed to look like an Italian village, this warehouse-like complex once provided the royal palaces with food and other supplies.

Today the estate houses the Bornstedt Buffalo brewery and distillery, which delivers fine brews and (sometimes) schnapps, as it has since 1689. The brewpub's restaurant is a good place for lunch, serving local specialties (€10-20 plates). The kid-friendly grounds also house a wood-fired bakery with fresh bread and pastries. You can watch hatmakers, candlemakers, coopers, potters, and glassmakers produce (and sell) their wares using traditional techniques.

Cost and Hours: Free except during special events, Mon-Fri 12:00-18:00, Sat-Sun 11:00-18:00, restaurant serves food until 22:00, Ribbeckstrasse 6, tel. 0331/550-650, www.krongut-bornstedt.de.

Getting There: From Sanssouci, walk toward the windmill, then follow the street to the right (An der Orangerie) about 500 yards.

MORE SIGHTS IN POTSDAM

Potsdam Town

The easy-to-stroll town center has pedestrianized shopping streets lined with boutiques and eateries. For a small town, this was a cosmopolitan place: Frederick the Great imported some very talented people. For example, Dutch merchants and architects built the Dutch Quarter (Holländisches Viertel, at the intersection of Leiblstrasse and Benkertstrasse) with gabled red-brick buildings that feel like a little corner of Amsterdam. The city also has a good film museum and a museum of Prussian history (both near Breite Strasse). Even if you're just racing through Potsdam on your way to the palaces, you can still catch a glimpse of the town center by riding bus #695 or #606 (described earlier, under "Getting Around Potsdam"). Skip Potsdam's much-promoted Wannsee boat rides, which are exceedingly dull.

Cecilienhof

This former residence of Crown Prince William was the site of the historic Potsdam Conference in the summer of 1945. During these meetings, Harry Truman, Winston Churchill, and Joseph Stalin negotiated how best to punish Germany for dragging Europe through another devastating war. It was here that the postwar map of Europe was officially drawn, setting the stage for a protracted Cold War that would drag on for four-and-a-half decades.

Designed to appear smaller and more modest than it actually is, Cecilienhof pales in comparison to the grand palaces concentrated around Sanssouci Park; it's only worth visiting if you're a WWII or Cold War history buff (or would like to visit the nearby Meierei brewpub).

Cost and Hours: €6, includes audioguide, April-Oct Tue-Sun 10:00-18:00, Nov-March Tue-Sun 10:00-17:00, closed Mon year-round, tel. 0331/969-4200, www.spsg.de.

Getting There: Ride the bus to the Reiterweg stop, at the northern end of Potsdam (from Sanssouci Palace, take bus #695; from the train station, ride tram #92 or #96). At Reiterweg, transfer to bus #603 (toward Höhenstrasse), and get off at the Schloss Cecilienhof stop.

Eating: Try the brewery called **Meierei** ("Creamery") behind the palace at Cecilienhof. Its nice beer garden offers spectacular views of the lake, solid German food, and great homemade beer. When you walk down the hill into the restaurant, note the big open field to the right—it used to be part of the Berlin Wall (€6-15 meals with table service, €3 bratwurst in self-service beer garden, Tue-Sun 12:00-22:00, closed Mon, follow *Meierei* signs to Im Neuen Garten 10, tel. 0331/704-3211).

Babelsberg

Movie buffs might already know that the nearby suburb of Babelsberg (just east of Potsdam) hosts the biggest film studio in Germany, where classics such as *The Blue Angel* and *Metropolis,* as well as more recent hits *The Reader* and *Inglourious Basterds,* were filmed (for visitor information, see www.filmpark-babelsberg.de).

Sachsenhausen Concentration Camp Memorial

About 20 miles north of downtown Berlin, the small town of Oranienburg was the site of one of the most notorious Nazi concentration camps. Sachsenhausen's proximity to the capital gave it special status as the place to train camp guards and test new procedures. It was also the site of the Third Reich's massive counterfeiting operation, depicted in the Oscar-winning 2007 movie *The Counterfeiters.* Today Sachsenhausen, worth ▲▲, is open to visitors as a memorial and a mu-

seum (Gedenkstätte und Museum Sachsenhausen), honoring the victims and survivors, and teaching visitors about the atrocities that took place here.

GETTING THERE

Take a train to the town of Oranienburg (20-50 minutes); from there, it's a quick trip by bus or taxi to the camp, or a 20-minute walk. The whole journey takes just over an hour each way.

From downtown Berlin, a regional **train** speeds from the Hauptbahnhof to Oranienburg (hourly, 25 minutes). Or you can take the S-Bahn (S-1) line from various stops downtown, including Potsdamer Platz, Brandenburger Tor, Friedrichstrasse, and Oranienburger Strasse (3/hour, 45-50 minutes depending on starting point). Note that the slower S-Bahn may not necessarily take longer if you factor in the time it takes to get to the Hauptbahnhof, find the correct platform, and wait for your connecting train. The S-1 line also goes southward to Potsdam—making it possible to connect Sachsenhausen and Potsdam's palaces in one extremely busy day.

Once at the Oranienburg train station, the **bus** to the memorial departs from lane 4, right in front of the station (on weekdays the hourly #804 is timed to meet most regional trains but runs only every 2 hours on weekends, direction: Malz; bus #821 also possible but only 5/day, direction: Tiergarten; €1.30, covered by Berlin transit day pass for zones ABC, get off at Gedenkstätte stop). You can also take a **taxi** (€6, ask for the *Gedenkstätte*—geh-DENK-steh-teh).

Otherwise, it's a 20-minute **walk** to the memorial: Turn right out of the train station and head up Stralsunder Strasse for about two blocks. Turn right under the railroad trestle onto Bernauer Strasse, following signs for *Gedenkstätte Sachsenhausen*. At the traffic light, turn left onto André-Pican-Strasse, which becomes Strasse der Einheit. After two blocks, turn right on Strasse der Nationen, where you'll pass a memorial stone commemorating the death march. This leads right to the camp, where you enter the grounds through the gaps in the wall.

ORIENTATION

Cost and Hours: Free, mid-March-mid-Oct Tue-Sun 8:30-18:00, mid-Oct-mid-March Tue-Sun 8:30-16:30; avoid visiting on Mon, when the grounds and visitors center are open but the exhibits inside the buildings are closed; Strasse der Nationen 22.

Information: The visitors center has WCs, a bookshop, and a helpful information desk. The map in this book is sufficient to navigate the camp, but the €0.50 map sold at the visitors center

NEAR BERLIN

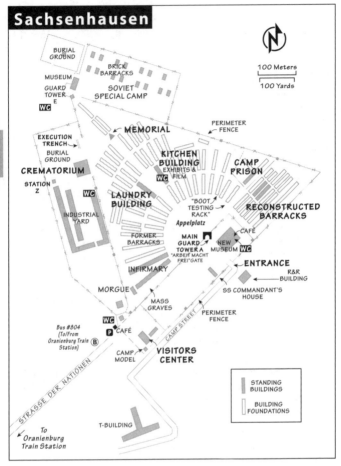

is probably worth getting for the extra background information it includes. I'd skip the €3 audioguide (which includes the map) even if it were free: Its five hours of slow commentary are unnecessary, given the ample English information posted within the camp. Tel. 03301/2000, www.gedenkstaette-sachsenhausen.de.

Tours from Berlin: While you can visit Sachsenhausen on your own, a tour helps you understand the camp's complicated and important story. Virtually all walking-tour companies in Berlin offer side-trips to Sachsenhausen. You'll meet in the city, then ride together by train to Oranienburg, and walk to the camp. The round-trip takes about six hours, much of which is spent in transit—but the time that you spend at the camp is made very meaningful by your guide's commentary.

Check the walking-tour companies' websites, or compare brochures to find an itinerary that fits your schedule. Options include **Original Berlin Walks** (€15, April-Oct Tue-Fri and Sun at 10:00, less frequent off-season) and **Insider Tour** (€15, Tue-Sun at 10:00). Warning: A few unscrupulous tour companies run trips to Sachsenhausen even on Mondays, when the grounds are technically "open," but all of the museum exhibits are closed.

Eating: Pack a lunch or buy lunch en route, as dining choices at the camp are minimal. The little "Info Café" inside the camp offers small snacks, and Bistro To Go, just outside the visitors center, serves basic fare (wurst, soup).

BACKGROUND

Completed in July of 1936, Sachsenhausen was the first concentration camp built under SS chief Heinrich Himmler. It was designed in the panopticon ("all-seeing") model popular in British prisons. The grounds were triangular so they could be observed from a single point, the main guard tower. The design was intended to be a model for other camps, but they soon discovered a critical flaw that prevented its widespread adoption: It was very difficult to expand without interfering with sight lines.

Sachsenhausen was not, strictly speaking, a "death camp" for the mass production of murder (like Birkenau); it was a labor camp, intended to wring hard work out of the prisoners. Many toiled in a brickworks, producing materials that were to be used in architect Albert Speer's grandiose plans for erecting new buildings all over Berlin.

Between 1936 and 1945, about 200,000 prisoners did time at Sachsenhausen; about 50,000 died here, while numerous others were transported elsewhere to be killed (in 1942, many of Sachsenhausen's Jews were taken to Auschwitz). Though it was designed to hold 10,000 prisoners, by the end of its functional life the camp had up to 38,000 people. In the spring of 1945, knowing that the Red Army was approaching, guards took 35,000 able-bodied prisoners on a death march, leading them into the forest for seven days and nights with no rations. Rather than "wasting" bullets to kill them, SS troops hoped that the prisoners would expire from exhaustion. On the eighth day, after 6,000 had already died, the guards abandoned the group in the wilderness, leaving them free. When Soviet troops liberated Sachsenhausen on April 22, 1945, they discovered an additional 3,000 prisoners who had been too weak to walk and were left there to die (all but 300 ended up surviving).

Just three months after the war, Sachsenhausen was converted into Soviet Special Camp No. 7 for the USSR's own prisoners. It was a notorious "silent camp," where prisoners would disappear—

allowed no contact with the outside world and their imprisonment officially unacknowledged. The prisoners were Nazis as well as anti-Stalin Russians. By the time the camp closed in 1950, 12,000 more people had died here.

In 1961, Sachsenhausen became the first former concentration camp to be turned into a memorial. The East German government created the memorial mostly for propaganda purposes, to deflect attention from the controversial construction of the Berlin Wall and to exalt the USSR as the valiant anti-fascist liberators of the camp and all of Germany.

Since the end of the DDR, Sachsenhausen has been redeveloped into a true memorial, with updated museum exhibits (scattered throughout the grounds in various buildings) and an emphasis on preservation—documenting and sharing the story of what happened here.

NEAR BERLIN

❍ SELF-GUIDED TOUR

The camp's various exhibits offer a lot more information than you probably have time to take in. This outline covers the key parts of your visit.

Entrance

In the courtyard next to the visitors center, a **model** of the camp illustrates its unique triangular layout, containing the prisoners' barracks. This allowed guards stationed in tower A (at the main gate) to see everything going on inside those three walls. Along the left (east) side of the triangle is the crematorium, called Station Z. (Camp guards joked that inmates entered the camp at A and exited at Z.) The smaller buildings outside the main triangle served as workshops, factories, and extra barracks that were added when the camp ran out of room.

Walk up the dusty lane called Camp Street. On the right is the SS officers' R&R building, nicknamed the **"Green Monster,"** where prisoners were dressed in nice clothes and forced to wait on their keepers. Officials mostly chose Jehovah's Witnesses for this

duty, because they had a strong pacifist code and could be trusted not to attempt to harm their captors.

A left turn through the fence takes you into the courtyard in front of **guard tower A.** The clock on the tower is frozen at 11:07—the exact time that the Red Army liberated the camp. The building on the right—misnamed the **"New Museum"**—has an interesting DDR-era stained-glass window inside, as well as temporary exhibits and a small café.

Go through the gate cruelly marked *Arbeit Macht Frei*— "Work will set you free."

Main Grounds

Entering the triangular field, you can see that almost none of the original buildings still stand. Following the war, locals salvaged the barracks here for much-needed building materials. Tracing the perimeter, notice the electric fence and barbed wire. A few feet in front of the wall is a gravel track called the **"neutral zone"**—any prisoner setting foot here would be shot. This became a common way for prisoners to attempt suicide. Guards quickly caught on: If they sensed a suicide attempt, they'd shoot to maim instead of kill. It was typical upside-down Nazi logic: Those who wanted to live would die, and those who wanted to die would live.

Every morning, after a 4:15 wake-up call, prisoners would scramble to eat, bathe, and dress in time to assemble in the **roll-call grounds** in front of the guard tower by 5:00. Dressed in their standard-issue uniforms—thin, striped pajamas and wooden clogs— prisoners would line up while guards, in long coats and accompanied by angry dogs, barked orders and accounted for each person, including those who had died in the barracks overnight. It could take hours, in any weather. One misbehaving prisoner would bring about punishment for all others. One day, after a prisoner escaped, SS officer Rudolf Höss (who later went on to run Auschwitz-Birkenau) forced the entire population of the camp to stand here for 15 hours in a foot of snow and subzero temperatures. A thousand people died.

To the far right from the entrance, the wooden **barracks** (containing good museum displays with English descriptions) are re-

constructed from original timbers. Barrack 38 focuses on the Jewish experience at Sachsenhausen, as well as the general mistreatment of German Jews under the Nazis (including anti-Semitic propaganda). Barrack 39 explains everyday life, with stories following 20 individual internees. You'll see how prisoners lived: long rows of bunks, benches for taking paltry meals, latrines crammed wall-to-wall with toilets, and communal fountains for washing. Inmates would jockey for access to these facilities. The strongest, meanest, most aggressive prisoners—often here because they had been convicted of a violent crime—would be named *Kapo,* the head of the barrack (to discourage camaraderie, the worst prisoners, rather than the best, were "promoted"). Like at many other camps, the camp leaders at Sachsenhausen ran a system of organized rape, whereby they brought in inmates from the women's-only Ravensbrück concentration camp and forced them to "reward good prisoners" at Sachsenhausen.

Next to the barracks is the camp prison, where political prisoners or out-of-line inmates were sent. It was run not by the SS, but by the Gestapo (secret police), who would torture captives to extract information. Other prisoners didn't know exactly what went on here, but they could hear screams from inside and knew it was no place they wanted to be. This was also where the Nazis held special hostages, including three Allied airmen who had participated in a bold escape from a Nazi prisoner-of-war camp (the basis for *The Great Escape;* they later managed to escape from Sachsenhausen as well, before being recaptured) and Joseph Stalin's son, Yakov Dzhugashvili, who had been captured during the fighting at Stalingrad. (The Nazis offered to exchange the young man for five German officers. Stalin refused, and soon after, Yakov died here under mysterious circumstances.) The cells contain exhibits about the prisoners and the methods used by their captors.

Just outside the back of the building stand three posts (out of an original 15) with iron pegs near the top. Guards would execute people by tying their hands behind their backs, then hanging them on these pegs by their wrists until they died—a medieval method called *strappado.*

Walk around the inner semicircle toward the buildings in the middle of the camp. On this **"boot-testing track,"** prisoners were forced to put on boots two sizes too small and walk in a circle on uneven ground all day, supposedly to "test" the shoes for fighting at Stalingrad.

The rectangles of stones show where each of the barrack buildings once stood. At the center, a marker represents the location of the gallows, where prisoners would be publicly executed as a deterrent to others.

Two buildings stand in the middle of the triangle. On the left is the **laundry building,** with special exhibits on topics such as Operation Bernhard, Sachsenhausen's counterfeiting ring. Nazi authorities created the world's largest counterfeiting operation by forcing inmates who were skilled forgers to create fake bills that would flood the US and British economies and devalue their currencies. The 2007 movie *The Counterfeiters* depicts the moral dilemma the prisoners faced: whether to create perfect fakes, and support the Nazi cause... or risk execution by intentionally doing bad work to sabotage the operation.

On the right is the kitchen building, with exhibits that trace the chronological history of the camp. You'll learn how Sachsenhausen was actually built by prisoners and see original artifacts, including the gallows, a bunk from the barracks, uniforms, and so on. There are also photos, quotes, and a 22-minute film. The basement walls feature some bizarre cartoons of vegetables preparing themselves to be eaten (these were drawn later by Soviets).

Memorial and Crematorium

Head back to the far end of the camp, which is dominated by the towering, 130-foot-tall, 1961 pro-communist DDR **memorial** to the victims of Sachsenhausen. The 18 triangles at the top are red, the color designated for political prisoners (to the communists, they were more worthy of honor than the other Nazi victims who died here). At the base of the monument, two prisoners are being liberated by a noble Soviet soldier. The prisoners are unrealistically robust, healthy, and optimistic (they will survive and become part of the proud Soviet proletariat!). The **podium** in front was used by the East German army for speeches and rallies—exploiting Sachsenhausen as a backdrop for their propaganda.

From here, head left and go through the gap in the fence to find the execution trench, used for mass shootings. When this system proved too inefficient, the Nazis built "Station Z,"

the nearby **crematorium,** where they could execute and dispose of prisoners more systematically. Its ruins are inside the white building (prior to the camp's liberation by Soviet troops, Nazi guards destroyed the crematorium to remove evidence of their crimes).

The crematorium's ramp took prisoners down into the "infirmary," while the three steps led up to the dressing room. This is where, on five occasions, the Nazis tested Zyklon-B (the chemical later responsible for killing hundreds of thousands at Auschwitz). Most of the building's victims died in the room with the double row of bricks (for soundproofing; the Nazis also blasted classical music to mask noise). Victims would report here for a "dental check," to find out if they had gold or silver teeth that could be taken. They would then stand against the wall to have their height measured—and a guard would shoot them through a small hole in the wall with a single bullet to the back of the skull. (The Nazis found it was easier for guards to carry out their duties if they didn't have to see their victims face-to-face.)

Bodies were taken to be incinerated in the ovens (which still stand). Notice the statue of the emaciated prisoner—a much more accurate depiction than the one at the DDR monument. Outside, a burial ground is filled with ashes from the crematorium.

The Rest of the Camp

Back inside the main part of the camp you can head left, up to the tip of the triangle (behind the big monument) to find a museum about the postwar era, when Sachsenhausen served as a **Soviet Special Camp.** Nearby is a burial ground for victims of that camp. At this corner of the triangle, the gate in the fence—called **tower E**—holds a small exhibit about the relationship between the camp and the town of Oranienburg.

Heading back toward the main guard tower, along the wall toward the front corner, are the long, green barracks of the **infirmary,** used for medical experiments on inmates (as explained by the exhibits inside). This was also where Soviet soldiers found the 3,000 remaining survivors when they liberated the camp. The small building in back was the morgue—Nazis used the long ramp to bring in the day's bodies via wheelbarrows. Behind that is a field with six stones, each marking 50 bodies for the 300 prisoners who died after the camp was freed.

While all of this is difficult to take in, as with all concentration camp memorials, the intention of Sachsenhausen is to share its story and lessons—and prevent this type of brutality from ever happening again.

PRACTICALITIES

This section covers just the basics on traveling in Germany (for much more information, see *Rick Steves Germany*). You'll find free advice on specific topics at www.ricksteves.com/tips.

Money

Germany uses the euro currency: 1 euro (€) = about $1.10. To convert prices in euros to dollars, add about 10 percent: €20 = about $22, €50 = about $55. (Check www.oanda.com for the latest exchange rates.)

The standard way for travelers to get euros is to withdraw money from ATMs (which locals call a *Geldautomat*) using a debit card, ideally with a Visa or MasterCard logo. Before departing, call your bank or credit-card company: Confirm that your card(s) will work overseas, ask about international transaction fees, and alert them that you'll be making withdrawals in Europe. Also ask for the PIN number for your credit card in case it'll help you use Europe's "chip-and-PIN" payment machines (see below); allow time for your bank to mail your PIN to you. To keep your valuables safe, wear a money belt.

Dealing with "Chip and PIN": Much of Europe—including Germany—is adopting a "chip-and-PIN" system for credit cards, and some merchants rely on it exclusively. European chip-and-PIN cards are embedded with an electronic chip, in addition to the magnetic stripe used on our American-style cards. This means that your credit (and debit) card might not work at payment machines, such as those at train and subway stations, toll roads, parking garages, luggage lockers, and self-serve gas pumps. Major US banks are beginning to offer credit cards with chips, but many of these are chip-and-signature cards, for which your signature (not your PIN) verifies your identity. In Europe, these cards should work for live transactions and at most payment machines, but probably won't work for offline transactions such as at unattended gas pumps. If a payment machine won't take your card, look for a machine that takes cash or see if there's a cashier nearby who can manually process your transaction. Often the easiest solution is to pay for your purchases with cash you've withdrawn from an ATM using your debit card (Europe's ATMs still accept magnetic-stripe cards).

Dynamic Currency Conversion: If merchants or hoteliers offer to convert your purchase price into dollars (called dynamic currency conversion, or DCC), refuse this "service." You'll pay more in fees for the expensive convenience of seeing your charge in dollars. If an ATM offers to "lock in" or "guarantee" your conversion rate, choose "proceed without conversion." Other prompts might state, "You can be charged in dollars: Press YES for dollars, NO for euros." Always choose the local currency.

Staying Connected

Smart travelers call ahead or go online to double-check tourist information, learn the latest on sights (special events, tour schedules, and so on), book tickets and tours, make reservations, reconfirm hotels, and research transportation connections.

To call Germany from the US or Canada: Dial 011-49 and then the area code (minus its initial zero) and local number. (The 011 is our international access code, and 49 is Germany's country code.)

To call Germany from a European country: Dial 00-49 followed by the area code (minus its initial zero) and local number. (The 00 is Europe's international access code.)

To call within Germany: If you're dialing from a phone number within the same area code (for example, from a local landline), just dial the local number. If you're calling outside your area code (for example, from a mobile phone), dial both the area code (which starts with a 0) and the local number.

To call from Germany to another country: Dial 00 followed by the country code (for example, 1 for the US or Canada), then the area code and number. If you're calling European countries whose phone numbers begin with 0, you'll usually have to omit that 0 when you dial.

Tips: Local phone numbers in Germany can have different numbers of digits within the same city or even the same business. Mobile phone numbers start with 015, 016, or 017. Some numbers, typically those that start with 018 (including some train and airline information numbers), are premium toll calls.

Traveling with a mobile phone—whether an American one that works in Germany, or a European one you buy upon arrival—is handy, but can be pricey. If you bring your own phone, consider

From:	rick@ricksteves.com
Sent:	Today
To:	info@hotelcentral.com
Subject:	Reservation request for 19-22 July

Dear Hotel Central,

I would like to reserve a room for 2 people for 3 nights, arriving 19 July and departing 22 July. If possible, I would like a quiet room with a double bed and a bathroom inside the room.

Please let me know if you have a room available and the price.

Thank you!
Rick Steves

getting an international plan; most providers offer a global calling plan that cuts the per-minute cost of phone calls and texts, and a flat-fee data plan.

Use Wi-Fi whenever possible. Most hotels and many cafés offer free Wi-Fi, and you'll likely also find it at tourist information offices, major museums, and public-transit hubs. With Wi-Fi you can use your smartphone to make free or inexpensive domestic and international calls via a calling app such as Skype, FaceTime, or Google+ Hangouts. When you can't find Wi-Fi, you can use your cellular network to connect to the Internet, text, or make voice calls. When you're done, avoid further charges by manually switching off "data roaming" or "cellular data."

It's possible to stay connected without a mobile phone. To make cheap international calls from your hotel-room phone, you can buy an international phone card. These work with a scratch-to-reveal PIN code, allow you to call home to the US for pennies a minute, and also work for domestic calls. Calling from your hotel-room phone without using an international phone card is usually expensive.

You can still find public pay phones in post offices and train stations. Avoid using an international phone card at a German pay phone—a surcharge effectively eliminates any savings. For more on phoning, see www.ricksteves.com/phoning.

Making Hotel Reservations

I recommend reserving rooms in advance, particularly during peak season. For the best rates, book directly with the hotel using their official website (not a booking agency's site). If there's no secure reservation form, or for complicated requests, send an email with the following information: number and type of rooms; number of nights; arrival date; departure date; and any special requests. (For a sample form, see the sidebar.) Use the European style for writing dates: day/month/year. Hoteliers typically ask for your credit-card number as a deposit. Some cities require hoteliers to charge a daily tourist tax; in Berlin, it's 5 percent of the room rate.

Some hotels are willing to deal to attract guests: Try emailing several hotels to ask for their best price. In general, hotel prices can soften if you do any of the following: offer to pay cash, stay at least three nights, or travel off-season.

Eating

At mealtime, there are many options beyond restaurants. For hearty, stick-to-the-ribs meals—and plenty of beer—look for a beer hall *(Bräuhaus)* or beer garden *(Biergarten)*. *Gasthaus, Gasthof, Gaststätte,* and *Gaststube* all loosely describe an informal, inn-type eatery. A *Kneipe* is a bar, and a *Keller* (or *Ratskeller*) is a restaurant or tavern located in a cellar. A *Schnell Imbiss* is a small fast-food takeaway stand. Department-store cafeterias are also common and handy.

The classic German dish is sausage *(Wurst)*. The hundreds of varieties are usually served with mustard *(Senf)*, a roll *(Semmel)* or pretzel *(Breze)*, and sauerkraut. The generic term *Bratwurst* (or *Rostbratwurst*) simply means "grilled sausage." To enjoy a *Weisswurst*—a boiled white Bavarian sausage made of veal—peel off the skin and eat it with sweet mustard. *Currywurst* comes with a delicious curry-infused ketchup. You'll also find schnitzel everywhere (pork is cheaper than veal). Salads are big, leafy, and good. Germans are passionate about choosing organic products—look for *Bio.*

Ethnic eateries—such as Italian, Turkish, Greek, and Asian—are good values. Shops and stands selling Turkish-style *Döner Kebab* (gyro-like, pita-wrapped rotisserie meat) are also common.

In Germany, good service is relaxed (slow to an American). When you want the bill, say, *"Rechnung* (REHKH-noong), *bitte."* To tip for good service, it's customary to round up around 10 percent. Rather than leave coins on the table (considered slightly rude), do as the locals do: When the server comes by with the bill, simply hand over paper money, stating the total you'd like to pay. For example, if paying for a €10 meal with a €20 bill, while handing your money to the server, say "Eleven, please" (or *"Elf, bitte"* if you've got your German numbers down). The server will keep a €1 tip and give you €9 in change.

Germany has both great wine *(Wein)* and beer *(Bier)*. Order wine *süss* (sweet), *halb trocken* (medium), or *trocken* (dry). For beer, *dunkles* is dark, *helles* or *Lager* is light, *Flaschenbier* is bottled, and *vom Fass* is on tap. *Pils* is barley-based, and *Weizen, Hefeweizen,* or *Weissbier* is yeasty and wheat-based. *Berliner Weisse* is Berlin's fizzy, slightly sour brew, often sweetened with a shot of syrup. When you order beer, ask for *eine Halbe* for a half-liter (though it's not always available) or *eine Mass* for a whole liter (about a quart).

Transportation

By Train: German trains—speedy, comfortable, and fairly punctual—cover cities and small towns well. Faster trains (such as the high-speed ICE) are more expensive than slower "regional" trains. To see if a rail pass could save you money—which is often the case in Germany—check www.ricksteves.com/rail. If buying point-to-point tickets, note that prices can fluctuate (you can usually save money by booking more expensive train journeys online; tickets are sold up to three months in advance). To research train schedules and fares, visit Germany's excellent online timetable, www.bahn.com.

By Bus: While most American travelers find the train to be the better option, ultra-low-fare long-distance buses are worth considering. The main bus operators are MeinFernBus (http://meinfernbus.de), FlixBus (www.flixbus.de), and Berlin Linien Bus (www.berlinlinienbus.de).

By Car: It's cheaper to arrange most car rentals from the US. For tips on your insurance options, see www.ricksteves.com/cdw, and for route planning, consult www.viamichelin.com. Bring your driver's license.

Germany's toll-free autobahn (freeway) system lets you zip around the country in a snap. While there's often no official speed limit, going above the posted recommended speed invalidates your insurance. Many German cities—including Munich, Freiburg, Frankfurt, Cologne, Dresden, Leipzig, and Berlin—require drivers to buy a special sticker *(Umweltplakette)* to drive in the city center. These come standard with most German rental cars; ask when you pick up your car. A car is a worthless headache in cities—park it safely (get tips from your hotel).

Local road etiquette is similar to that in the US. Ask your car-rental company for details, or check the US State Department website (www.travel.state.gov, search for your country in the "Learn about your destination" box, then click on "Travel and Transportation").

Helpful Hints

Emergency Help: To summon the **police** or an **ambulance**, call 112. For passport problems, call the **US Embassy** (in Berlin, tel. 030/83050, consular services tel. 030/8305-1200—Mon–Thu 14:00–16:00 only) or the **Canadian Embassy** (in Berlin, tel. 030/203-120). For other concerns, get advice from your hotel.

Theft or Loss: To replace a passport, you'll need to go in person to an embassy (see above). Cancel and replace your credit and debit cards by calling these 24-hour US numbers collect: Visa—tel. 303/967-1096, MasterCard—tel. 636/722-7111, American Express—tel. 336/393-1111. In Germany, to make a collect call to the US, dial 0800-225-5288. Press zero or stay on the line for an English-speaking operator. File a police report either on the spot or within a day or two; you'll need it to submit an insurance claim for lost or stolen rail passes or travel gear, and it can help with replacing your passport or credit and debit cards. Precautionary measures can minimize the effects of loss—back up your digital photos and other files frequently. For more information, see www.ricksteves.com/help.

Time: Germany uses the 24-hour clock. It's the same through 12:00 noon, then keep going: 13:00, 14:00, and so on. Germany, like most of continental Europe, is six/nine hours ahead of the East/West Coasts of the US.

Business Hours: In Germany, most shops are open from about 9:00 until 18:00 or 20:00 on weekdays, but close early on Saturday (generally between 12:00 and 17:00, depending on whether you're in a town or a big city). In small towns, a few shops may take a mid-afternoon break on weekdays (roughly between 12:00 and 14:00 or 15:00). Throughout Germany, most shops close entirely on Sundays.

Holidays and Festivals: Germany celebrates many holidays, which can close sights and attract crowds (book hotel rooms ahead). For more on holidays and festivals, check Germany's website: www.germany.travel. For a simple list showing major—though not all—events, see www.ricksteves.com/festivals.

Numbers and Stumblers: What Americans call the second floor of a building is the first floor in Europe. Europeans write dates as day/month/year, so Christmas 2016 is 25/12/16. Commas are decimal points and vice versa—a dollar and a half is 1,50, and there are 5.280 feet in a mile. Germany uses the metric system: A kilogram is 2.2 pounds; a liter is about a quart; and a kilometer is six-tenths of a mile.

Resources from Rick Steves

This Snapshot guide is excerpted from my latest edition of *Rick Steves Germany*, which is one of many titles in my ever-expanding series of guidebooks on European travel. I also produce a public television series, *Rick Steves' Europe*, and a public radio show, *Travel with Rick Steves*. My website, www.ricksteves.com, offers free travel information, a forum for travelers' comments, guidebook updates, my travel blog, an online travel store, and information on European rail passes and our tours of Europe. If you're bringing a mobile device on your trip, you can download my free Rick Steves Audio Europe app, featuring podcasts of my radio shows, my Best of Berlin City Walk audio tour, and travel interviews about Germany. You can get Rick Steves Audio Europe via Apple's App Store, Google Play, or the Amazon Appstore. For more information, see www.ricksteves.com/audioeurope. You can also follow me on Facebook, Twitter, and Instagram.

Additional Resources
Tourist Information: www.germany.travel
Passports and Red Tape: www.travel.state.gov
Packing List: www.ricksteves.com/packing
Travel Insurance: www.ricksteves.com/insurance
Cheap Flights: www.kayak.com
Airplane Carry-on Restrictions: www.tsa.gov
Updates for This Book: www.ricksteves.com/update

How Was Your Trip?
If you'd like to share your tips, concerns, and discoveries after using this book, please fill out the survey at www.ricksteves.com/feedback. Thanks in advance—it helps a lot.

German Survival Phrases

In the phonetics, ī sounds like the long i in "light," and bolded syllables are stressed.

English	German	Pronunciation
Good day.	Guten Tag.	**goo**-tehn tahg
Do you speak English?	Sprechen Sie Englisch?	**shprehkh**-ehn zee **ehgn**-lish
Yes. / No.	Ja. / Nein.	yah / nīn
I (don't) understand.	Ich verstehe (nicht).	ikh fehr-**shtay**-heh (nikht)
Please.	Bitte.	**bit**-teh
Thank you.	Danke.	**dahng**-keh
I'm sorry.	Es tut mir leid.	ehs toot meer līt
Excuse me.	Entschuldigung.	ehnt-**shool**-dig-oong
(No) problem.	(Kein) Problem.	(kīn) proh-**blaym**
(Very) good.	(Sehr) gut.	(zehr) goot
Goodbye.	Auf Wiedersehen.	owf **vee**-der-zayn
one / two	eins / zwei	īns / tsvī
three / four	drei / vier	drī / feer
five / six	fünf / sechs	fewnf / zehkhs
seven / eight	sieben / acht	**zee**-behn / ahkht
nine / ten	neun / zehn	noyn / tsayn
How much is it?	Wieviel kostet das?	**vee**-feel **kohs**-teht dahs
Write it?	Schreiben?	**shrī**-behn
Is it free?	Ist es umsonst?	ist ehs oom-**zohnst**
Included?	Inklusive?	in-kloo-**zee**-veh
Where can I buy / find...?	Wo kann ich kaufen / finden...?	voh kahn ikh **kow**-fehn / **fin**-dehn
I'd like / We'd like...	Ich hätte gern / Wir hätten gern...	ikh **heh**-teh gehrn / veer **heh**-tehn gehrn
...a room.	...ein Zimmer.	īn **tsim**-mer
...a ticket to ___.	...eine Fahrkarte nach ___.	ī-neh **far**-kar-teh nahkh
Is it possible?	Ist es möglich?	ist ehs **mur**-glikh
Where is...?	Wo ist...?	voh ist
...the train station	...der Bahnhof	dehr **bahn**-hohf
...the bus station	...der Busbahnhof	dehr **boos**-bahn-hohf
...the tourist information office	...das Touristen-informations-büro	dahs too-**ris**-tehn-in-for-mah-see-**ohns**-**bew**-roh
...the toilet	...die Toilette	dee toh-**leh**-teh
men	Herren	**hehr**-rehn
women	Damen	**dah**-mehn
left / right	links / rechts	links / **rehkhts**
straight	geradeaus	geh-**rah**-deh-ows
What time does this open / close?	Um wieviel Uhr wird hier geöffnet / geschlossen?	oom **vee**-feel oor veerd heer geh-**urf**-neht / geh-**shloh**-sehn
At what time?	Um wieviel Uhr?	oom **vee**-feel oor
Just a moment.	Moment.	moh-**mehnt**
now / soon / later	jetzt / bald / später	yehtst / bahld / **shpay**-ter
today / tomorrow	heute / morgen	**hoy**-teh / **mor**-gehn

PRACTICALITIES

In a German Restaurant

PRACTICALITIES

English	German	Pronunciation
I'd like / We'd like...	Ich hätte gern / Wir hätten gern...	ikh **heh**-teh gehrn / veer **heh**-tehn gehrn
...a reservation for...	...eine Reservierung für...	ī-neh reh-zer-**feer**-oong fewr
...a table for one / two.	...einen Tisch für eine Person / zwei Personen.	ī-nehn tish fewr ī-neh pehr-zohn / tsvī pehr-**zoh**-nehn
Non-smoking.	Nichtraucher.	**nikht**-rowkh-er
Is this seat free?	Ist hier frei?	ist heer frī
Menu (in English), please.	Speisekarte (auf Englisch), bitte.	**shpī**-zeh-kar-teh (owf **ehng**-lish) **bit**-teh
service (not) included	Trinkgeld (nicht) inklusive	**trink**-gehlt (nikht) in-kloo-**zee**-veh
cover charge	Eintritt	**ī**n-trit
to go	zum Mitnehmen	tsoom **mit**-nay-mehn
with / without	mit / ohne	mit / **oh**-neh
and / or	und / oder	oont / **oh**-der
menu (of the day)	(Tages-) Karte	(**tah**-gehs-) **kar**-teh
set meal for tourists	Touristenmenü	too-**ris**-tehn-meh-**new**
specialty of the house	Spezialität des Hauses	**shpayt**-see-ah-lee-**tayt** dehs **how**-zehs
appetizers	Vorspeise	**for**-shpī-zeh
bread / cheese	Brot / Käse	broht / **kay**-zeh
sandwich	Sandwich	**zahnd**-vich
soup	Suppe	**zup**-peh
salad	Salat	zah-**laht**
meat	Fleisch	flīsh
poultry	Geflügel	geh-**flew**-gehl
fish	Fisch	fish
seafood	Meeresfrüchte	**meh**-rehs-**frewkh**-teh
fruit	Obst	ohpst
vegetables	Gemüse	geh-**mew**-zeh
dessert	Nachspeise	**nahkh**-shpī-zeh
mineral water	Mineralwasser	min-eh-**rahl**-vah-ser
tap water	Leitungswasser	**lī**-toongs-vah-ser
milk	Milch	milkh
(orange) juice	(Orangen-) Saft	(oh-**rahn**-zhehn-) zahft
coffee / tea	Kaffee / Tee	kah-**fay** / tay
wine	Wein	vīn
red / white	rot / weiß	roht / vīs
glass / bottle	Glas / Flasche	glahs / **flah**-sheh
beer	Bier	beer
Cheers!	Prost!	prohst
More. / Another.	Mehr. / Noch eins.	mehr / nohkh īns
The same.	Das gleiche.	dahs **glīkh**-eh
Bill, please.	Rechnung, bitte.	**rehkh**-noong **bit**-teh
tip	Trinkgeld	**trink**-gehlt
Delicious!	Lecker!	**lehk**-er

For more user-friendly German phrases, check out *Rick Steves' German Phrase Book and Dictionary* or *Rick Steves' French, Italian & German Phrase Book.*

INDEX

INDEX

INDEX

Explore Europe

At ricksteves.com you can browse through thousands of articles, videos, photos and radio interviews, plus find a wealth of money-saving travel tips for planning your dream trip. And with our mobile-friendly website, you can easily access all this great travel information anywhere you go.

TV Shows

Preview the places you'll visit by watching entire half-hour episodes of Rick Steves' Europe (choose from all 100 shows) on-demand, for free.

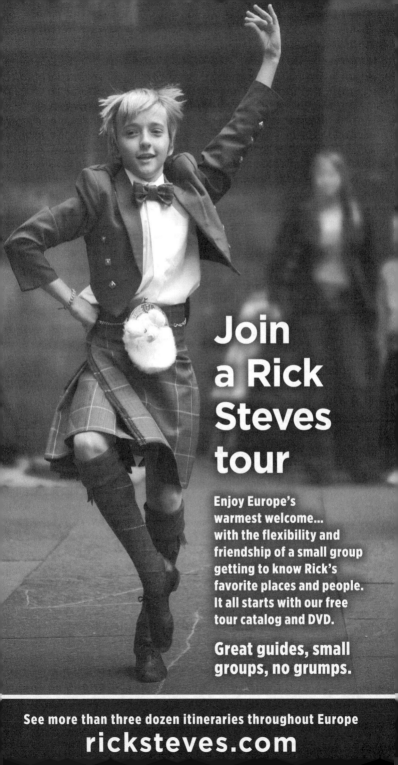

Free information and great gear to

▸ Explore Europe

Browse thousands of articles, video clips, photos and radio interviews, plus find a wealth of money-saving tips for planning your dream trip. You'll find up-to-date information on Europe's best destinations, packing smart, getting around, finding rooms, staying healthy, avoiding scams and more.

▸ Travel News

Subscribe to our free Travel News e-newsletter, and get monthly updates from Rick on what's happening in Europe!

▸ Travel Forums

Learn, ask, share—our online community of savvy travelers is a great resource for first-time travelers to Europe, as well as seasoned pros.

Rick Steves' Europe Through the Back Door, Inc.

turn your travel dreams into affordable reality

▶ Rick's Free Audio Europe™ App

The Rick Steves Audio Europe™ app brings history and art to life. Enjoy Rick's audio tours of Europe's top museums, sights and neighborhood walks—plus hundreds of tracks including travel tips and cultural insights from Rick's radio show—all organized into geographic playlists. Learn more at ricksteves.com.

▶ Great Gear from Rick's Travel Store

Pack light and right—on a budget—with Rick's custom-designed carry-on bags, wheeled bags, day packs, travel accessories, guidebooks, journals, maps and Blu-ray/DVDs of his TV shows.

130 Fourth Avenue North, PO Box 2009 • Edmonds, WA 98020 USA
Phone: (425) 771-8303 • Fax: (425) 771-0833 • ricksteves.com

Save time and energy

This guidebook is your independent-travel toolkit. But for all it delivers, it's still up to you to devote the time and energy it takes to manage the preparation and logistics that are essential for a happy trip. If that's a hassle, there's a solution.

Rick Steves Tours

A Rick Steves tour takes you to Europe's most interesting places with great

with minimum stress

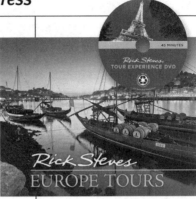

guides and small groups of 28 or less. We follow Rick's favorite itineraries, ride in comfy buses, stay in family-run hotels, and bring you intimately close to the Europe you've traveled so far to see. Most importantly, we take away the logistical headaches so you can focus on the fun.

customers—along with us on 40 different itineraries, from Ireland to Italy to Istanbul. Is a Rick Steves tour the right fit for your travel dreams? Find out at ricksteves.com, where you can also get Rick's latest tour catalog and free Tour Experience DVD.

Join the fun

This year we'll take 18,000 free-spirited travelers— nearly half of them repeat

Europe is best experienced with happy travel partners. We hope you can join us.

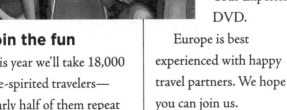

See our itineraries at ricksteves.com

Maximize your travel skills with a good guidebook.

TRAVEL CULTURE

Europe 101
European Christmas
Postcards from Europe
Travel as a Political Act

eBOOKS

Nearly all Rick Steves guides are available as ebooks. Check with your favorite bookseller.

RICK STEVES' EUROPE DVDs

12 New Shows 2015–2016
Austria & the Alps
The Complete Collection 2000-2016
Eastern Europe
England & Wales
European Christmas
European Travel Skills & Specials
France
Germany, BeNeLux & More
Greece, Turkey & Portugal
The Holy Land: Israelis & Palestinians Today
Iran
Ireland & Scotland
Italy's Cities
Italy's Countryside
Scandinavia
Spain
Travel Extras

PHRASE BOOKS & DICTIONARIES

French
French, Italian & German
German
Italian
Portuguese
Spanish

PLANNING MAPS

Britain, Ireland & London
Europe
France & Paris
Germany, Austria & Switzerland
Ireland
Italy
Spain & Portugal

Photo © Patricia Feaster

Avalon Travel
a member of the Perseus Books Group
1700 Fourth Street
Berkeley, CA 94710

Printed in Canada by Friesens. First printing January 2016.

ISBN 978-1-63121-463-9

For the latest on Rick's lectures, guidebooks, tours, public radio show, and public
television series, contact Rick Steves' Europe, 130 Fourth Avenue North, Edmonds,
WA 98020, 425/771-8303, www.ricksteves.com, rick@ricksteves.com.

Rick Steves' Europe

Special Publications Manager: Risa Laib
Managing Editor: Jennifer Madison Davis
Editors: Glenn Eriksen, Tom Griffin, Katherine Gustafson, Suzanne Kotz, Cathy Lu,
John Pierce, Carrie Shepherd
Editorial & Production Assistant: Jessica Shaw
Editorial Intern: Chelsea Wing
Researchers: Sandra Hundacker, Robyn Stencil, Gretchen Strauch, Cary Walker
Contributor: Gene Openshaw
Maps & Graphics: David C. Hoerlein, Sandra Hundacker, Lauren Mills, Mary Rostad

Avalon Travel

Senior Editor and Series Manager: Madhu Prasher
Editor: Jamie Andrade
Associate Editors: Sierra Machado and Maggie Ryan
Copy Editor: Patrick Collins
Proofreaders: Megan Mulholland and Suzie Nasol
Indexer: Stephen Callahan
Production & Typesetting: Rue Flaherty, Tabitha Lahr, and Jane Musser
Cover Design: Kimberly Glyder Design
Maps & Graphics: Kat Bennett, Mike Morgenfeld

Photo Credits

Front Cover: Berlin Cathedral (Berliner Dom) © Olena Buyskykh/123rf.com
Title Page Photo: View of the French Cathedral and the Konzerthaus at
Gendarmenmarkt © Heike Jestram/www.123rf.com
Additional Photography: Dominic Arizona Bonuccelli, Ben Cameron, Lisa Friend,
Cameron Hewitt, David C. Hoerlein, Sandra Hundacker, Gene Openshaw, Rhonda
Pelikan, Rick Steves, Gretchen Strauch, Ragen Van Sewell, Ian Watson, Matt
Yglesias, Wikimedia Commons—PD-Art/PD-US. Photos are used by permission
and are the property of the original copyright owners.

More for your trip!
Maximize the experience with Rick Steves as your guide

Guidebooks
Switzerland, Vienna, and Prague guides make side-trips smooth and affordable

Phrase Books
Rely on Rick's German Phrase Book & Dictionary

Rick's TV Shows
Preview where you're going with 4 shows on Germany

Free! Rick's Audio Europe™ App
Hear Germany travel tips from Rick's radio shows

Small Group Tours
Including the Best of Germany, Austria and Switzerland

For all the details, visit ricksteves.com

ABOUT THE AUTHOR

RICK STEVES

 Since 1973, Rick Steves has spent 100 days every year exploring Europe. Along with writing and researching a best-selling series of guidebooks, Rick produces a public television series *(Rick Steves' Europe),* a public radio show *(Travel with Rick Steves),* a blog (on Facebook), and an app and podcast *(Rick Steves Audio Europe);* writes a nationally syndicated newspaper column; organizes guided tours that take over 20,000 travelers to Europe annually; and offers an information-packed website (www.ricksteves.com). With the help of his hardworking staff of 100 at Rick Steves' Europe—in Edmonds, Washington, just north of Seattle—Rick's mission is to make European travel fun, affordable, and culturally enlightening for Americans.

Connect with Rick:

facebook.com/RickSteves   twitter: @RickSteves

instagram: ricksteveseurope